ZONDERVAN

FRESH VOICES

A COLLECTION

OF BESTSELLERS

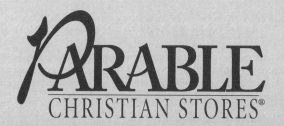

PARABLE

CHRISTIAN STORES®

ZONDERVAN™

Fresh Voices
Copyright © 2003 by Zondervan

Excerpts are included from the following books:

Rumors of Another World
Copyright © 2003 by SCCT

The God I Love
Copyright © 2003 by Joni Eareckson Tada

The Case for a Creator
Copyright © 2004 by Lee Strobel

Breakthrough Prayer
Copyright © 2003 by Jim Cymbala

Going Public with Your Faith
Copyright © 2003 by Walt Larimore and Bill Peel

Every Child Needs a Praying Mom
Copyright © 2003 by Fern Nichols

When God Doesn't Answer Your Prayer
Copyright © 2004 by Gerald L. Sittser

Boundaries Face to Face
Copyright © 2003 by Henry Cloud and John Townsend

NIV Student Bible—Large Print
Copyright © 2003 by Zondervan

The Purpose-Driven® Life
Copyright © 2002 by Rick Warren
Illustrations Copyright © 2002 by Michael Halbert

Requests for information should be addressed to:

Zondervan, *Grand Rapids, Michigan 49530*

Printed in the United States of America

03 04 05 06 07 08 09 /❖ DC/ 10 9 8 7 6 5 4 3 2 1

Contents

Foreword

If you love books, then you are holding something special. *Fresh Voices* is a collection of writings from today's most talented Christian authors. We created this sampler because the list of new books releasing during the fall of 2003 and winter of 2004 is the largest in Zondervan's seventy-two-year history. Never before have so many major books from so many best-selling Zondervan authors arrived in a single season.

We want you to sample some of the great Christian literature about to arrive at your favorite bookstore, whether it is Lee Strobel's explaining new scientific evidence for God in *The Case for a Creator,* Joni Eareckson Tada's inspiring you with God's great faithfulness in her memoir *The God I Love,* or Philip Yancey's revealing clues to the supernatural in *Rumors of Another World.*

Zondervan's mission is to be the leading Christian communications company meeting the needs of people with resources that glorify Jesus Christ and promote biblical principles. We know the books featured in *Fresh Voices* will meet many needs. Please let us know if they meet yours. Which book did you like best? Did one help a seeking friend or relative? Write us at zpub@zondervan.com. We may read your message at a Zondervan employee meeting and together celebrate how God uses books to change lives.

Greg Stielstra
Director of Marketing
for Trade Books

PHILIP YANCEY

rumors
OF ANOTHER WORLD

WHAT
ON
EARTH
ARE
WE
MISSING?

I wrote this book for people who live in the borderlands of belief, a phrase first suggested to me by the writer Mark Buchanan. In regions of conflict, such as the Korean peninsula, armies on both sides patrol their respective borders, leaving a disputed territory in between as a buffer zone. Wander into that middle area and you'll find yourself in a "no-man's-land" belonging to neither side.

In matters of faith, many people occupy the borderlands. Some give church and Christians a wide berth yet still linger in the borderlands because they cannot set aside the feeling that there must be a spiritual reality out there. Maybe an epiphany of beauty or longing gives a nudge toward something that must exist beyond the everyday routine of life—but what? Big issues—career change, the birth of a child, the death of a loved one—raise questions with no easy answers. Is there a God? A life after death? Is religious faith only a crutch, or a path to something authentic?

I also meet Christians who would find it difficult to articulate why they believe as they do. Perhaps they absorbed faith as part of their upbringing, or perhaps they simply find church an uplifting place to visit on weekends. But if asked to explain their faith to a Muslim or an atheist, they would not know what to say.

What would I say? That question prompted this book. I wrote it not so much to convince anyone else as to think out loud in hopes of coming to terms with my own faith. Does religious faith make sense in a world of the Hubble telescope and the Internet? Have we figured out the basics of life, or is some important ingredient missing?

To me, the great divide separating belief and unbelief reduces down to one simple question: Is the visible world around us all there is? Those unsure of the answer to that question—whether they approach it from the regions of belief or unbelief—live in the borderlands. They wonder whether faith in an unseen world is wishful thinking. Does faith delude us into seeing a world that doesn't exist, or does it reveal the existence of a world we can't see without it?

I "think out loud" by putting words on paper, and out of that process this book emerged. I begin with the visible world around us, the world all of us inhabit. What rumors of another world might it convey? From there, I look at the apparent contradictions. If this is God's world, why doesn't it look more like it? Why is this planet so messed up? Finally, I consider how two worlds—visible and invisible, natural and supernatural—might interact and affect our daily lives. Does the Christian way represent the best life on this earth or a kind of holding pattern for eternity?

I am at times a reluctant Christian, plagued by doubts and "in recovery" from bad church encounters. I have explored these experiences in other books, and so I determined not to mine my past yet again in this one. I am fully aware of all the reasons not to believe. So then, why do I believe? Read on.

Philip Yancey

paying attention

Master of beauty, craftsman of the snowflake, inimitable contriver,
endower of Earth so gorgeous & different from the boring Moon,
thank you for such as it is my gift.

JOHN BERRYMAN

A short story by the Spanish writer Carmen Corde tells of a young
woman who gives birth to a blind son. "I do not want my child
to know that he is blind!" she informs family and neighbors, for-
bidding anyone to use telltale words such as "light," "color," and
"sight." The boy grows up unaware of his disability until one day a
strange girl jumps over the fence of the garden and spoils everything by using all the forbidden words. His world shatters in the
face of this unimagined new reality.

In modern times, Christians resemble the strange girl who
brings a message from outside. To a skeptical audience they bring
rumors of another world beyond the fence, of an afterlife beyond
death, of a loving God who is somehow working out his will in the
chaotic history of this planet. As in Carmen Corde's story, the news
may not be welcome. "We forget that what is to us an extension of
sight is to the rest of the world a peculiar and arrogant blindness,"
the Catholic novelist Flannery O'Connor admitted.

I have found that living with faith in an unseen world requires
constant effort. After all, the "garden" in which we live, the natural
world, conceals as much about God as it reveals. The Westminster Catechism teaches that the primary purpose of life is "to glorify God, and
to enjoy him forever." But how does that well-honed answer translate
into actual day-to-day living, especially when the God we are supposed to enjoy and glorify remains elusive and hidden from view?

As a start, I can aim to make daily life *sacramental*, which
means literally to keep the sacred (*sacra*) in mind (*mental*). In other

9

words, I seek a mindfulness—a mind full—of God's presence in the world. I have no desire to escape the natural world, the pattern of gnostics, desert monks, and fundamentalists who flee "worldliness." Nor do I deny the supernatural, the error of the reducers. Rather, I want to bring the two together, to reconnect life into the whole that God intended.

This world, all of it, either belongs to God or it does not. As Meister Eckhart said, "If the soul could have known God without the world, the world would never have been created." If I take seriously the sacred origin of this world, at the very least I must learn to treat it as God's work of art, something that gave God enormous pleasure. "God saw all that he had made, and it was very good," Genesis reports.

I think of a piece of art, a sculpture, given to me by a friend this year. I made a shelf to display it prominently, in the best light. Often I stop to admire it and point it out to guests. Clearly, modern society is not treating creation as God's work of art. We pave over fertile land for parking lots, pump toxins into the sky and rivers, and mindlessly cast species into extinction. Our treatment of human beings follows suit: We allow 24,000 children to die each day of preventable diseases and abort 126,000 more, house families in cardboard shacks and under bridges, and manufacture weapons capable of exterminating most of humanity. And as the Body Worlds exhibit made clear, the way some people treat their own bodies also shows deep disrespect for God's masterpiece.

At the same time, we tend to confine the sacred to a fenced-in area, the "spiritual," reserved for church activities. Many people rarely give God a thought apart from an hour on Sunday morning, when they sing songs of praise, listen to a sermon, and then reenter the secular world as if passing through an air lock. My pastor tells me that church members tell off-color jokes in the parking lot that they would never repeat in the sanctuary. When the doors close behind them, they believe they leave sacred space, as if the world neatly divides between secular and sacred.

Blaise Pascal, who achieved renown both for his mathematics and his devotional writings, suggests another approach, of seeing the natural world as a foreshadowing of the supernatural. "He has done in the bounties of nature what He would do in those of grace, in order that we might judge that He could make the invisible, since He made the visible excellently." Beauty abounds in nature: A collection of seashells, the castoff excretions of lowly mollusks, is probably the most beautiful artwork in my home. And I need only read the Psalms to realize that God wants us to love and honor him through the creation, not apart from it.

Celtic spirituality speaks of "thin places" where the natural and supernatural worlds come together at their narrowest, with only a thin veil between them. I have visited places where nature's works speak loudly of their creator: bald eagles and beluga whales in Alaska, coral and tropical fish on the Great Barrier Reef off Australia, exotic birds and butterflies at Angel Falls in Venezuela, seashells on the beaches of Kenya. Each of these memories stands out as a highlight of a year, each involved a major logistical effort, and periodically I review the memories in thick photo albums that hardly do justice to what I experienced. One day I realized with a start that God "sees" all the wonders of the earth at all times. Not only does God see them, God is their source, and each reveals something of the Creator.

A year ago a friend stopped by Colorado on a farewell tour. She was going blind, doctors had told her, and in preparation she was revisiting her favorite places so that when the darkness descended they would live on in her mind. For her, as for me, beauty is a strong pointer to God. She was, in effect, storing away a memory bank of grace.

The first step in being mindful is to accept my creaturely state. Frankly, I find that process much easier now that I live in Colorado. When I climb a mountain, I sense my status as creature immediately. My self-importance recedes. In Chicago, surrounded by high-rise buildings, I could look out my window and see people dining in restaurants, standing in line at cash machines, jogging or rollerblading, commuting to work, shopping, walking their babies in strollers. We humans design cities for our own convenience, and while living there it was easy to assume the world was about *us*. City lights dimmed the stars, and manmade structures shut out my view of the natural world. Climbing a mountain, everything changes.

A few years ago, hikers in the Rocky Mountains found a herd of two hundred elk killed by a freak ball of lightning. Photos from a helicopter show their swollen bodies arranged in a random pattern among thousands of trees blown over by the explosive force. I think of that scene sometimes when I scramble down a trail above timberline, glancing every few seconds at an angry thunderhead closing in. An old climber once observed that mountains are neither fair nor unfair, they just simply sit there. Perhaps, but when I am standing on an exposed ledge, enveloped in immensity, vulnerable to hail, blizzards, lightning, and other dangers, I feel very small and very fragile. Any hubris I picked up living in a city melts away. Nature reminds me how dependent and frail I am, how mortal.

"Too late I have loved you, O beauty so ancient and so new," Augustine laments in *The Confessions*. He proceeds to describe a time in his life when he allowed things of beauty to seduce him away from God their maker. Later, he returned to "those fair things" and at last traced the sunbeams to their source. I find that I too must consciously track that source, must "hallow" the world around me.

One night in Costa Rica I joined a guided expedition to a government reserve in order to observe a natural phenomenon: giant leatherback turtles laying their eggs. The guide used a red-filtered flashlight so as not to disorient the turtles, and at midnight we trudged for almost a mile along the beach, its sand still warm from the day's sun, until we found a female preparing her nest.

The turtle reached down in soft sand, one muscular flipper at a time, to scoop out and then fling the sand behind her. As she worked her way down, each scoop required more and more effort. The sand got wet and heavy, and she had to fling it above the rim of the hole she was digging. Eventually she reached a depth of three feet, her body fully submerged in sand. Now, each flinging of sand thrust her whole body to the side, and despite her best efforts much of the sand still fell back in the trench. She scooped it up again and slung it toward the surface.

We tourists, from Germany, Holland, Costa Rica, and the U.S., stood in silence late into the night, spellbound, watching this primordial drama. The crashing surf made a rhythmic soundtrack, and silvery clouds drifted over the moon. The mother turtle heaved and gasped, her mouth opening and closing like a fish laboring to breathe. Finally, after an hour's hard work, the trench satisfied her and she began to drop shiny white eggs the size of billiard balls. They glistened in the moonlight, gelatinous. We counted at least sixty. The last few eggs were smaller—also infertile, said the guide, so that if predators uncovered her nest, these would go first.

Her task accomplished, the leatherback clambered slowly out of the nest and began a forty-five-minute process of filling it in with sand. Her powerful front flippers, made dexterous by separate "fingers," could toss sand ten feet behind her. She filled the trench, tamped the sand delicately, as with loving care, added more on top, packed it too, then made a wide circle of disturbed sand to confuse any predators. Exhausted, she lumbered off, dragging herself on the sand and resting after every three to four strokes, toward the sea. We watched as the smallest waves, their foam glowing in the moonlight, pushed her back repeatedly toward shore. At last she gained the strength to lunge past the waves, dipped her head beneath the surface, and disappeared.

The guide informed us that the mother turtle weighed almost a ton and was probably a hundred years old. (Many used to live past two hundred, before deep dragnets on the shrimp boats started entangling them and the population dwindled.) The largest reptiles on earth, leatherbacks don't even breed for the first sixty years, and of course the mother never sees the results of her efforts. When the babies hatch, they burrow to the surface and make a mad dash to the sea, with only a third surviving the onslaught of coyotes, raccoons, and seagulls. The sea poses many more dangers, and few of the baby turtles live to lay eggs themselves. Those who do will unfailingly return in sixty years to the same beach in Costa Rica, one of only three beaches frequented by leatherbacks.

Revisiting the site the following morning, I could barely make out the camouflaged nest. Tracks like those made by a large-wheeled all-terrain vehicle (ATV) led from the nest to the sea. The mother turtle's flippers had made the rounded furrows, and between them I noticed a much more shallow one made by her dragging tail.

I sat on a piece of driftwood and thought of the immensity of the world within the sea. How little of creation do we humans understand, much less control: the wonders of instinctual behavior, the rhythms of nature that go on whether any humans observe them or not, the comparative smallness of human beings. I made a conscious choice to turn the memory of the previous night into an act of gratitude, even worship. It had put me in my place.

Five hundred years ago the Renaissace scholar Pico della Mirandola delivered an oration that defined the role of humanity in creation. After God had created the animals, all the essential roles had been filled, but "the Divine Artificer still longed for some creature which might comprehend the meaning of so vast an achievement, which might be moved with love at its beauty and smitten with awe at its grandeur." To contemplate and appreciate all the rest, to revere and to hallow, to give mute creation a voice of praise— these were the roles reserved for the species made in God's image.

The great French entomologist Jean Henri Fabre climbed the same six-thousand-foot mountain more than forty times because of the perspective it gave him on his work and on humanity. He said, "Life has unfathomable secrets. Human knowledge will be erased from the archives of the world before we possess the last word that the Gnat has to say to us." Not to mention the turtle.

Along with many Christians, I have undergone two conversions: first from the natural world to discover the supernatural, and later to rediscover the natural from a new viewpoint. For some, the second conversion comes almost without effort. Gerard Manley Hopkins lived in a world "charged with the grandeur of God," and St. Francis treated not just birds and beasts but the sun and moon as his beloved siblings. As the Egyptian saint Pachomius, leader of seven thousand monks in the fourth century, observed, "The place in the monastery which is closest to God is not the church, but the garden. There the monks are at their happiest."

In his writings, naturalist John Muir made virtually no division between the natural and supernatural. He named as one of his life's two greatest moments the time he found the rare Calypso orchid blooming in a Canadian swamp (the other was when he camped with Ralph Waldo Emerson at Yosemite). Muir loved God's creation so fiercely that he said with remorse, "it is a great comfort ... that vast multitudes of creatures, great and small and infinite in number, lived and had a good time in God's love before man was created."

For me, though, the second conversion has not come without struggle. I have sampled the glories of the natural world, yes—even finding the rare Calypso orchid blooming among ferns on the hill behind my home—and have also tasted of the grace and goodness of God. How, though, do I bring the two worlds together? The mixed messages in nature confuse me, its beauties so often commingled with brutality and pain.

"Are not two sparrows sold for a penny? Yet not one of them will fall to the ground apart from the will of your Father," promised Jesus. "And even the very hairs of your head are all numbered. So don't be afraid; you are worth more than many sparrows." Yet sparrows still fall to the ground, as do the hairs from chemotherapied human heads; and of sixty leatherback turtles born, only two or three survive. A sovereign God who wills against his ultimate will, who superintends a universe of a hundred billion galaxies and yet lavishes intimate attention on its tiny creatures—how do I comprehend such a God?

Sometimes I rail against the mysteries and sometimes I accept them. As a starting point, I take for granted that a creature's proper response to God is humility. Accepting creatureliness may require that I, like Job, bow before a master plan that makes no apparent sense.

In the face of doubt, I have learned the simple response of considering the alternatives. If there is no Creator, what then? I would have to view the world with all its suffering as well as all its beauty as a random product of a meaningless universe, the briefest flare of a match in cosmic darkness. Perhaps the very sense that *something is wrong* is itself a rumor of transcendence, an inbuilt longing for a healed planet on which God's will is done "on earth as it is in heaven."

"Remember your Creator in the days of your youth, before the days of trouble come," warned the Teacher of Ecclesiastes in the pangs of foreboding over old age and death. His book chronicles a systematic search for an alternative, a life apart from a Creator. In the end, he found that both hedonism and despair lead to a vexing sense of meaninglessness. "Fear God and keep his commandments, for this is the whole duty of man," the Teacher concluded, in words reminiscent of the Westminster Shorter Catechism.

Astonishingly, the Creator seldom imposes himself on his creatures. It requires attention and effort on our part to "remember your Creator," because the Creator slips quietly backstage. God does not force his presence on us. When lesser gods attract, God withdraws, honoring our fatal freedom to ignore him.

Isaac Luria, a Hasidic mystic of the eighteenth century, proposed a system known as *zimsum* to explain the existence of suffering and evil as well as how God relates to his creation. To make room for the material world, God had to pull himself back and concede space, the space necessary for something other than God to exist. God poured his own essence in the form of light into holy vessels, which in turn would pour it down on the creation.

God's voluntary withdrawal, however, made possible the emergence of opposing forces, including evil. A cosmic catastrophe occurred, introducing confusion into creation. Some of the sparks of God's light returned to their source; what remained within the broken vessels, or "husks," fell onto every animal, vegetable, and mineral part of the world.

The resulting creation, said Luria, now shields God's holy light, hiding it from view. Or, in another metaphor, creation retains the "smell" of God as a wineskin retains the smell of wine. Skeptical, unseeing people can even deny that God exists. Believers have the task of releasing the holy sparks from the husks. We do so through a process of "hallowing," and all of us have a part to play in this process.

Other theologians have refined Luria's thoughts, and from them I learn that hallowing is a deliberate, ongoing process. I do not gain a new set of supernatural eyes that enable me suddenly to see the world with perfected vision. Every day, every hour, every moment, I must exercise my calling to hallow God's creation, whether it be leatherback turtles in Costa Rica or the irritating kid next door who peppers my yard with golf balls. Holy sparks are potentially trapped in every moment of my day, and as God's agent I am called to release them.

John Calvin urged his followers to heed a "universal rule, not to pass over, with ungrateful inattention or oblivion, those glorious perfections which God manifests in his creatures."* To abide by that rule requires a training of spiritual senses akin to how naturalists develop their physical senses.

In the town where I live, an elderly couple leads the local chapter of the National Audobon Society. Bill eats too much, has had numerous surgeries, and walks with a cane. Sylvia strikes you as a kindly soul who spends the day knitting and baking cookies for Bill and the grandchildren. Yet when I accompany them on birding expeditions, their trained ears and eyes put mine to shame. Within three notes they identify a bird call and can usually point to the bird in question in seconds. I can walk through a wetland area and see nothing; they peer behind the twigs and leaves to the wildlife hidden inside.

I am working on improving my senses in both the natural world and the more artificial world we human beings have constructed around us. From my home in Colorado, a parade of God's creation marks the passing of the day. I begin the day reading and sipping coffee in a solarium. In the summer, broad-tailed hummingbirds appear first, zooming in like Harrier jets only to brake, hover, and extend their long tongues to slurp sugar-water from their feeder. Out another window hangs a bird feeder full of sunflower seeds. (It more resembles a miniature space ship because of all the squirrel deterrents I've added to it.) Small birds that nest in neighboring trees stop by first: three varieties of nuthatches, chickadees, pine siskins, an occasional goldfinch bright as the morning sun. Then larger birds home in for a snack: black-headed and evening grosbeaks, Stellar jays, Cassin's finches, hairy and downy woodpeckers.

---

*In *The Imitation of Christ* Thomas à Kempis says, "If your heart were right, then every created thing would be a mirror of life, and a book of sacred doctrine. There is no creature so small and worthless that it does not show forth the goodness of God." He adds one caution about the natural world, that we not cling "to anything created with unmeasured affection."

The woodpeckers have beaks designed for drilling wood, not for plucking sunflower seeds out of a container, and as a result they scatter seeds like small hailstones on the ground below. That attracts the squirrels. First come the common brown squirrels, and soon their mountain cousins pay a visit. These, the Abert squirrels, are solid black with reddish eyes and tufted ears that give them a diabolical look. They spend half an hour or so chasing the brown squirrels away before finally settling down to feast on the fallen seeds. Next a red fox shows up. He stalks behind the same rock every morning, a routine the Abert squirrels know well. After a few feints and a futile charge, he usually gives up and trots away, with the squirrels loudly clucking their disdain.

Eight times I have watched the fox catch a squirrel. Once I saw a hawk dive out of the sky and pluck a pygmy nuthatch off the feeder. It then sat on a woodpile and turned its head from side to side, glaring, as its talons squeezed out the tiny bird's life. I've watched a doe and her two spotted fawns take halting, stiff-legged steps toward the birdbath for a drink. Herds of elk wander through the yard to feast on our carefully tended shrubs and flowers. A bear once climbed the deck and pawed for the feeder until I shouted him away. Skunks and raccoons make nighttime appearances. Some years, a marmot takes up residence in a culvert at the end of the driveway.

Sitting behind glass in a heated house, I have a daily sense that I am the impostor on this scene. I have little trouble believing that this is God's world in which I am blessed to live. "Beauty and grace are performed whether or not we will sense them," writes Annie Dillard. "The least we can do is try to be there."

In downtown Chicago my day proceeded very differently. Most mornings began with a run through the park. I saw few animals, other than squirrels and pigeons, unless I chose a route through the Lincoln Park Zoo. I saw instead winos and homeless people sleeping under newspapers and smelly blankets; prostitutes sleeping in doorways next to discarded condoms; well-dressed yuppies standing in neat lines at the bus stops; foreign-born nannies pushing the carriages of those yuppies' children; garbagemen, janitors, street sweepers, sewer workers, and others who perform the undesirable jobs that keep a city running.

These too are God's holy sparks, I had to remind myself. More, these creations harbor not just God's sparks but his very own image. He created them in order to reflect back something of himself, a privilege assigned to no other part of creation. And what did I do then, what do I do now, to release those holy sparks, to polish the mirror that reflects back God's image?

When I moved to Chicago, it took a while for me to adjust to the background noise of Clark Street. Lying in bed in the summer with windows open, I heard buses growling and wheezing down the street, sirens in the distance, the crash of bottles being thrown into a Dumpster behind a late-night bar, the throbbing bass from speakers in a car stopped at a red light. I thought I would never adjust, until one night I barely noticed. The sounds had dissolved into a kind of white noise.

When I moved to Colorado, I had to adjust to silence. The slightest noise jerked me awake. I started when the refrigerator kicked on and when steam made the heating pipes clank. I began to wonder what else I had become deaf to during my time in Chicago.

I learned a lesson about paying attention from an eccentric orchestra conductor, a year when the Romanian musician Sergiu Celibidache paid a visit to Chicago with his Munich Philharmonic. Few orchestras would work with Celibidache because he demands twelve to eighteen rehearsals before every performance, compared to four for most orchestras. He insists on an Eastern approach to music: striving not so much to recapitulate an "ideal" performance by some other conductor and orchestra, but rather to create an engrossing encounter with music at the moment. He refuses to listen to recordings or even to allow taping of his own performances: How can you reproduce on a flat disk something heard in a concert hall with walls and cushioned seats and human bodies modifying the sound? "Like peas, music cannot be canned," he says.

Celibidache made his first trip to the U.S. at age seventy-one, and when I heard him, five years later, he needed assistance mounting the podium. He chose familiar pieces for the concert, but, oh, what a difference. He ignored the tempo markings by the composer, stretching out Mussorgsky's *Pictures at an Exhibition* to twice its normal length. Considering one phrase and the next, he seemed far more interested in drawing out the tonal quality of a given passage than incorporating that passage in the onward march of the piece. He approached the music more like meditation than performance.

I missed the precision of the Chicago Symphony yet heard the music as a revelation, or series of revelations, with individual moments more important than the whole. At the end the audience rose to their feet and applauded for twelve minutes. Celibidache had every soloist, duet, and orchestral section stand, and bowed to them.

A concertmaster who played under Celibidache said, "His whole concept is that every phrase has a shape and it comes from one phrase and leads to another. He feels that there is a truth in music, and it should be discovered." A critic likened his concerts to religious rites over which the conductor presides as a high priest. Celibidache himself says, "How does this piece go? No idea. We'll have to find out. Emptiness is the highest form of concentration."

Our very bodies react when we pay attention. At Orchestra Hall I leaned forward, moved my head from one side to the other, cupped my hands behind my ears, closed my eyes. A poet, Simone Weil says, encounters beauty by intensely fixing attention on something real. So does a lover. Can I do something similar in the inner life, with God? I need not always search for new insights, new truths: "The most commonplace truth when it floods the *whole soul,* is like a revelation."

I realized, on reflection, that I tend to approach life as a sequence rather than as a series of moments. I schedule my time, set goals, and march onward toward their achievement. Phone calls, or any unscheduled event, I view as a jarring interruption. How different from the style of Jesus, who often let other people—interruptions—determine his daily schedule. He gave full attention to the person before him, whether it be a Roman officer or a nameless woman with a hemorrhage of blood. And he drew lasting spiritual lessons from the most ordinary things: wildflowers, wheat crops, vineyards, sheep, weddings, families.

In the movie *Awakenings,* Robert DeNiro portrays one of the patients of Dr. Oliver Sacks, who discovered the near-miraculous powers of the drug L-DOPA on patients suffering from severe Parkinsonism and an encephalitic sleeping-sickness disease. Some of these patients had lived in a rigid, almost frozen state for years, even decades, unable to speak or communicate. The new drug acted on their brains in such a way that their bodies loosened up, and instead of sitting immobile like statues all day they "awakened" to new life.

DeNiro delighted in the simplest actions. He could rise from his wheelchair and take a walk, deciding on a whim whether to turn to the left or the right. He could speak and respond in ways that others could notice. He could touch another person. In a poignant scene, the whole ward came to life, going out on the town, dancing together, listening to music, then returned to the ward as the drug wore off to resume their catatonic states.

Sacks's case studies give detailed reports of individual patients. Some could not cope with the new realities; Rose R., "frozen" for forty-three years, felt herself in a dizzying time warp. Others, such as Leonard L., embraced the new world joyfully. "I feel saved," he said, with tears of joy on his face—"resurrected, reborn. I feel a sense of health amounting to Grace." He read Dante's *Paradiso,* visited Manhattan at night, touched flowers and leaves with astonished delight, typed a 50,000 word autobiography in three weeks. Tragically, as happened with most of the patients, the effects of L-DOPA faded and after five months Leonard regressed to his former condition.

Reading the heartrending accounts of Sacks's patients, I understood the secret of the mystics, those we know as saints. They live one moment at a time. Perhaps that is why so many head into the desert or wilderness: it facilitates extreme attention.

If you can live through a moment, you can live through a day, and how you live a day is eventually how you live your life. I spend so much energy on the correct way to live in general that I miss the specific moments that are actually the only way I can live. Joan Chittister, a modern Benedictine, gives the corrective I need:

> [We must] hold every isolated thing in high regard whatever their use, to treat them gently, to take care of them well whatever their age. It leads us to become part of the holiness of the universe by recognizing each and every element of it as a spark of the Divine....
>
> We are part of a holy universe, not its creators and not its rulers. God has done the creating, God does the judging, and God waits for us to realize that....
>
> Everything we are, everything that is said to us, everything that happens to us is some kind of call from God. In fact, everything that happens is God's call to us either to accept what we should not change or to change what we should not accept so that the Presence of God can flourish where we are....
>
> Finding God is a matter of living every minute of life to its ultimate.

The goal of contemplation is to see life as God sees it, a unity of two worlds and not a division. That encompasses both a lifetime of practice and rare, single flashes of revelation.

"There is nothing unclean of itself," said the apostle Paul; and again, "So whether you eat or drink or whatever you do, do it all for the glory of God." To him, a sacramental view of life had everything to do with *direction*. Nature, people, eating, work, worship—everything in daily life points up the chain of a reordered world toward God. To ignore sexual, personal, social, professional, even political concerns would diminish the reality of God's presence in the world. When Paul touched on each area, he placed it in the order ordained by its Creator.

The reducer looks down for his or her instructions: Edward Wilson standing over an anthill with his magnifying glass scouting clues to human behavior. From that perspective, we use other people in order to enhance ourselves, because only the fittest survive. We follow the instinct of lust to perpetuate our genes. We exploit nature for our own use. We act altruistically with calculation, as a strategy.

A seeker of the sacred looks up, tracing the rays of sun back to their source. For Dante, the power of adolescent sexuality awakened in him awe and fear, and he looked to God, not his own body, for guidance on how to respond. For John Muir, nature expressed the brilliance of a master Artist, to whom he responded with gratitude and worship. For Mother Teresa, the dying beggars in the streets of Calcutta shrouded holy light, and though it helped the least fit to survive, she served them as if she were serving Christ himself. The Celtic saint Columba learned to experience God's presence everywhere: "At times plucking crabs from the rocks; at times fishing; at times giving food to the poor; at times in a solitary cell."

Biology is destiny, concludes the one who looks down. The prospects are bleak, for according to psychologists our impulses include a natural urge to murder our fathers and mothers, at least an occasional tendency to laziness and idleness, a penchant for cruelty and vulgarity.

Eternity is destiny, concludes the one who looks up. Our genes may indeed contain predispositions toward bestial instincts, but we hear a call to rise above them. You could stare at an anthill a long time before coming up with this list of qualities: love, joy, peace, patience, kindness, goodness, faithfulness, gentleness, and self-control. Yet Paul holds these up as proof of the presence of God in a person's life, the "fruit of the Spirit." Where God lives, those qualities flourish.

All of life involves a clash between impulse and inhibition, between our fallen nature and the image of God. A sacred view of life calls for simple trust that the One who created the human creature has our ultimate good in mind.

We are all of us more mystics than we believe or choose to believe.... We have seen more than we let on, even to ourselves. Through some moment of beauty or pain, some subtle turning of our lives, we catch glimmers at least of what the saints are blinded by; only then, unlike the saints, we go on as though nothing has happened. To go on as though something has happened, even though we are not sure what it was or just where we are supposed to go with it, is to enter the dimension of life that religion is a word for.

FREDERICK BUECHNER

SOURCES

9. *Berryman*: John Berryman, "Eleven Addresses to the Lord," no. 2, in *Love & Fame* (New York: Farrar, Straus & Giroux, 1970), 85.

9. *Corde*: Carmen Corde, quoted in Henri Nouwen, *¡Gracias!* (Maryknoll, N.Y.: Orbis, 1983), 74.

9. *O'Connor*: Flannery O'Connor, *Mystery and Manners* (New York: Farrar, Straus & Giroux, 1969), 180.

10. *Eckhart*: Meister Eckhart, Quoted in "Holy Fools," *Sojourners* (July 1994), 20.

10. *"God saw"*: Genesis 1:31.

10. *Pascal*: Blaise Pascal, *Pascal's Pensées* (New York: E. P. Dutton, 1958), 182.

12. *Augustine*: Augustine of Hippo, *The Confessions of St. Augustine* (Garden City, N.Y.: Image, 1960), 254.

14. *Mirandola*: Pico della Mirandola, "Oration on the Dignity of Man," available on numerous Internet sites including *http://history.hanover.edu/courses/excerpts/111pico.htm.*

14. *Fabre*: Jean Henri Fabre, *The Insect World of J. Henri Fabre* (Boston: Beacon, 1977), 326.

14. *Hopkins*: Gerard Manley Hopkins, "God's Grandeur," in *Poems and Prose of Gerard Manley Hopkins* (Baltimore: Penguin, 1953), 27.

14. *Pachomius*: Saint Pachomius, quoted in James Bryan Smith, *Embracing the Love of God* (San Francisco: HarperSanFrancisco, 1989), 138.

15. *Muir*: John Muir, *The Story of My Boyhood and Youth* (New York & Boston: Houghton Mifflin, 1913), 84.

15. *"Are not two sparrows"*: Matthew 10:29.

16. *"Remember your creator"*: Ecclesiastes 12:1.

16. *"Fear God"*: Ecclesiastes 12:13.

17. *Calvin*: John Calvin, *Institutes, I, xiv,* (Grand Rapids, Mich.: Eerdmans, 1964), 157.

18. *Dillard*: Annie Dillard, *Pilgrim at Tinker Creek* (New York: Harper's Magazine Press, 1974), 8.

19. *Celibidache*: Sergiu Celibidache, quoted in "Podium Paradox," in *Chicago Tribune* (April 16, 1989), Section 13, "Arts," 14–15.

20. *Weil*: Simone Weil, *Gravity & Grace* (New York: Routledge, 1995), 108, 105.

21. *Sacks*: Oliver Sacks, *Awakenings* (New York: Dutton, 1983), 67–79, 188–201.

22. *Chittister*: Joan Chittister, OSB., in James Martin, Ed., *How Can I Find God?* (Liguori, Mo.: Triumph, 1997), 85–86.

22. *"there is nothing"*: Romans 14:14 (kjv).

22. *"So whether"*: 1 Cor. 10:31.

23. *Columba*: from Adamnan's *Life of Saint Columba*, quoted in Robert Hudson and Shelley Townsend-Hudson, *Companions for the Soul* (Grand Rapids, Mich.: Zondervan, 1995), June 6 reading.

23. *"fruit of the Spirit"*: Galatians 5:22.

24. *Buechner*: Frederick Buechner, *A Room Called Remember* (San Francisco: HarperSanFrancisco, 1984), 152.

The GOD I LOVE

A MEMOIR

JONI EARECKSON TADA

A LIFETIME OF WALKING WITH JESUS

The smell of honeysuckle along the road near our farm . . . the sound of my parents' voices downstairs, talking sweet and soft above *The Perry Como Show* . . . the stirring of my young heart to words from the Bible . . . and the sight of a new day's sun sparkling over the waves near our beach camp. It was all a kid could hope for back in the '50s. Yet little did I know that God was wafting his fragrance in the honeysuckle, speaking to me through my parents' soft words, humbling me through every crash of each wave on the sand, and gently—ever so tenderly—wooing me to his side through all those Bible readings in Sunday school. I needed that. For not far off in the future, I would discover I needed God *desperately*. That's what *The God I Love* is all about. It's not so much a memoir; it's a memory still unfolding of the journey that keeps taking me deeper into the heart of my Savior, whether by walking or using a wheelchair. And it's my prayer that this story, which spans over fifty years, will resonate with each person who takes time to pick up the book . . . it's my prayer that *The God I Love* will serve as a roadmap, a guide, a signpost to light the journey of each reader, helping them to see their sweet, soft desperation of Jesus, too.

Joni Eareckson Tada

CHAPTER ONE

My son, preserve sound judgment and discernment, do not let them out of your sight; they will be life for you, an ornament to grace your neck. Then you will go on your way in safety, and your foot will not stumble; when you lie down, you will not be afraid; when you lie down, your sleep will be sweet.

Proverbs 3:21–24

I dug my toes into the sand of the Delaware beach, hugged my knees, and drew as close to the campfire as I could. The flames warmed our faces while behind us the night air chilled our backs. Huddled with my sisters and cousin, I smelled the burning logs and breathed in the fire's heat. We all sat in awe of my father. He stood across the campfire from us, a figure a-swirl in rising heat and smoke, his face underlit by flame as if he were a prophet on Mount Sinai. We clutched each other as he wove his story. And we didn't dare look over our shoulders toward the ocean, lest we catch sight of—

"The Flying Dutchman!"

My father's eyes widened as he fixed his gaze on us. "Just a few hundred yards across the water, he was, standing on the bow of his ship. He was so close I could see the glow of his pipe!"

The campfire crackled and popped, a burst of sparks twirling upward in the smoke. Another wave crashed on the sand, *shissh-SHING*, spilling its white foam over the ridge of the beach. Each wave edged closer to our campfire than the last one. Now I couldn't help myself. I peered over my shoulder, wondering if the Flying Dutchman's phantom schooner was out there, somewhere on the dark ocean.

"All the mates on board our ship had nearly given up," my father intoned. "Our vessel had been caught for five days in the Sargasso Sea. The thick seaweed had entwined our rudder and held us fast in its deadly grip. The water supply was gone, and our tongues were cracked and swollen. We knew our hope was spent when—"

"You saw the Dutchman," my sister whispered.

"Oh-*hoh*! you're a sharp lassie," Daddy commended.

We knew the legend by heart. It started on a wind-whipped, stormy night in the 1600s, when a Dutch sea captain steered his ship into the jaws of a gale at the Cape of Good Hope. The mounting waves hammered the vessel's sides, and the ship began to sink. As raging waters flooded the deck, the captain raised his fist and railed, "I *will* round this cape, even if I have to keep sailing until doomsday!"

As the legend goes, he did. And anyone who had the misfortune of sighting the old Flying Dutchman would surely die a terrible death. To this day, if you see the dark clouds of a gathering squall looming on the horizon, beware. You may spy the old Dutch sea captain smoking his pipe, and if you do, you too may seal your fate.

"But if you saw the Flying Dutchman when you were caught in the Sargasso Sea," one of us asked, "why didn't you die?"

We knew the answer. But we had to hear it again.

"Your daddy isn't afraid of any old curse," our father declared. "Why, I looked over the bow of our ship, and I spotted a great devil-fish. That gave me an idea."

I didn't know what a devil-fish was. But as Daddy spread his hands wide and flapped his arms, I knew it was something really big and powerful, like a giant manta ray. "I called for a harpoon," he gestured, "and waited for that devil-fish to float by. Slowly, I took aim—and I hurled the spear into his back!"

I grimaced.

"The great fish strained against the rope, but I held tight, calling for my shipmates. 'I say, *you*, Angus Budreau, and *you*, Georgy

Banks! Tie the end to the capstan!' They moved quickly while the fish pulled harder. 'Up with the foresail and mainsail and the mizzen! Set the jib and the flying jib!' I yelled.

"Slowly, our ship began to creak and groan. She was inching forward, pulled by the two-ton fish, straining and flapping his wing-fins with all his might. I could feel the weeds snapping beneath our hull—"

Our own muscles tightened at the mighty fish's effort—

"—and suddenly, we broke free. The sails began to flutter and fill with air. Finally, a gust caught the mainsail. The crew let out a cheer. Our ship was freed from the grip of the Sargasso Sea! As that tired old devil-fish sank into the murky depths, having spent his strength, we waved our sailor's caps farewell. And once again, we hit the high seas."

I felt sad that the devil-fish had to die. But I was glad my father had lived to tell the story. So was Mom—I could tell by the way she looked at him. I always searched her face after Daddy ended a story, to see whether the tale was true. She never gave anything away, though. She just stood up to throw another log on the fire. If one of us asked, "Mommy, is that true? Did that really happen?" she gave a sly grin. Maybe she didn't believe Daddy's stories as much as we did. But to her credit, she didn't let on. She always left us thinking there may be some truth to his tales, with her faithful answer: "Good story, Cap'n John!"

A burst of sparks exploded from the fire, and a gust scattered them in the night.

"There's his pipe!" someone cried. "I see the sparks!"

"No you don't."

"Yes I do!"

"Don't."

"Do!"

It went back and forth that way, *don't-do, don't-do*, until Mother stopped the motor, shushing, "Quiet, you girls."

"So, what happened to the Flying Dutchman?"

My father stood silent for a long moment. All was quiet except for the pounding of waves. Smoke and flames danced in the wind, causing shadows to flicker in all directions. Daddy slowly ventured a few steps toward the blackness that was the ocean, the stars, and the night. I grew nervous as he moved away from the well-lit safety of our campfire. He stopped, placed his hands on his hips, and peered into the distance as if searching for someone.

"I escaped the Dutchman," he said softly. "Not many do, but I was one of the blessed ones." My three sisters and our cousin, little Eddie, leaned forward to search the darkness too.

"Don't look too hard for that old seaman," Daddy warned, "for you may not be as fortunate as I was." His voice took on an ominous tone: "You may one day hear, 'Heh-heh-heh!'" With that, he turned around swiftly, rubbing his hands and snickering in sinister glee.

We squealed and grabbed onto one another, kicking sand to keep the ghost at bay. But the tale-teller was finished now. He gave a swooping bow, and we applauded generously.

"Please, *please* tell another one!" we chanted.

No, enough was enough. My father was always one to leave us hanging for more. I was glad for that. It made whatever else we did next sweeter. Like singing. When the stories ended, it was usually time for songs. Campfire songs, Girl Scout songs, hiking, sailing, or cowboy songs.

My mother and father crisscrossed more logs on the fire, creating an inferno, and we kids backed away our blankets. We had all spent the day digging for clams on the other side of the barrier island. The shallow, clear water of the Indian River inlet there concealed hundreds of fat clams just inches below the sand. The day's labor had been successful, and now our white-canvas Keds were lined up by the fire to dry out. My father's best friend—Uncle Eddie to us—ambled over and plopped a couple of ice buckets next to his son, little Eddie, "our cousin." They were filled with clams.

We each reached in and took one. Squinting our eyes against the heat of the campfire, we carefully placed the clams on the end of a log near enough to the flames to steam them. Soon the clams were bubbling around the edges. One by one, they popped open. Using our thumb and forefinger, we gingerly picked up a hot, half-opened shell, *ouch!*-ing and blowing on them until they cooled. We could hardly wait to get the clams, wet and salty, hot and chewy, into our mouths.

Daddy tilted his sailor's cap and began dancing a silly jig. He launched into a song written for him by an old sweetheart from his merchant marine days, in the early 1900s. It was a song to eat clams by.

> *I would not marry an oyster man, I'll tell you the reason why:*
> *His boots are always muddy, his shoes are never dry.*
> *A sailor boy, a sailor boy, a sailor boy 'twill be.*
> *Whenever I get married, a sailor's bride I'll be!*

Reaching farther down into the ice, past the clams piled on top, we pulled out fresh oysters. Our Uncle George, Daddy's brother, was in charge of knifing them open. This was one of those artful Maryland skills we hoped we too would one day excel in. It requires piercing the shell, heart, and muscle in a way that keeps the oyster plump and intact.

Uncle George passed out the opened oysters to us, and I held mine up, comparing its size to my sisters'. To hold in your hand the biggest and juiciest was a triumph in the art of gross. Balancing mine just so, I flattened my bottom lip, pressed the edge of the shell to it, tilted the oyster slightly, and slurped. I had seen some people swallow an oyster whole, but I preferred Daddy's way: chewing it. It tasted better that way, releasing a musty, salty flavor. The ritual never seemed odd when I was a child, but years later I would understand what people meant by the phrase "acquired taste."

Sea songs eventually gave way to cowboy songs, and then, when Daddy was sure we'd squeezed all the play we could from the evening, we sang hymns. Suddenly, the scene around the campfire was transformed from one of clam-slurping, sand-kicking, and tall-tale camaraderie into a sanctuary under the stars. The glowing sparks that rose now didn't come from a seaman's pipe, and the Atlantic Ocean no longer held fearful secrets of Davy Jones's Locker. Even the hissing foam of the retreating waves sounded soothing. Never was there a sweeter satisfaction than to lie back on a blanket, my hands under my head, and gaze at the starry dome above while singing a hymn.

I forgot all about tall tales as my father, full of warmth and tenderness, led us.

> *On a hill far away stood an old rugged cross,*
> *The emblem of suff'ring and shame;*
> *And I love that old cross where the dearest and best*
> *For a world of lost sinners was slain.*

We all joined in on the chorus. I loved adding harmony, fitting my notes under my parents' melody. We swelled the first part, like the flowing of the tide, and then sang gently on the last part, like the tide as it ebbed.

> *So I'll cherish the old rugged cross,*
> *Till my trophies at last I lay down;*
> *I will cling to the old rugged cross,*
> *And exchange it some day for a crown.*

As the rest of the family went on to the second verse, I stopped singing. I was listening to a larger song, one that came from the star-splattered heavens. With my knees bent heavenward, the fronts of my legs caught the heat and light of the campfire. A deep, cool shadow was cast over the rest of me as I lay listening to the universe drift by. Tiny clusters of stars and great constellations speckled the night, while the surf pounded away. The Atlantic Ocean was yet another universe of mysterious currents, touching the toes of Ireland and England, places too far away for me to believe they were real. And here we were, huddled around our small fire, a tiny ember on a beach stretching north and south for miles, with nary another camp in sight. We were a single point of light among thousands that night on the eastern seaboard, a coast on one of many continents, all on a planet dwarfed by galaxies spinning above.

I had never felt so small. Yet so safe.

Safe, secure, and significant. I couldn't imagine a kid anywhere else on the planet that night, much less among the sand dunes of the Delaware coast, who felt as safe as I. Part of that feeling was the stories. Most of it, the hymns. When someone started up, "I come to the garden alone, while the dew is still on the roses," I felt as though God himself were among us, illuminated by the fire and breathing a sigh with each wave.

My earliest recollections of being stirred by the Spirit happened through hymns. Soft, sweet, old hymns—the kind my Aunt Kitty liked to sing when she and Uncle George visited us on Friday nights, to go over the books from Daddy's business. Or the kind we sang at our little church in Catonsville. The sort of hymns we sang in the truck as we came over the Chesapeake Bay Bridge to the eastern shore, down Highway 1 through Queen Anne's County, over the bridge to the barrier island and our camping site. The same hymns whose words I knew by heart yet could not explain.

> *I know whom I have believ-ed and am persuaded*
> *That he is able to keep that which I've committed*
> *Unto him against that day.*

I treasured this family hymn, but as for its meaning, I was clueless. It didn't bother me that I couldn't grasp it. Five-year-olds are able to tuck words into cubbyholes in their hearts, like secret notes stored for a rainy day. All that mattered to me now was that these hymns bound me to the melody of my parents and sisters. The songs had something to do with God, my father, my family, and a small seed of faith safely stored in a heart-closet.

"Come on, everybody!" Daddy clapped his hands and roused us from our blankets. "Up on your feet and try this one."

> *Climb, climb up sunshine mountain, heavenly breezes blow*

We climbed the air and waved our hands hula-style—

> *Climb, climb up sunshine mountain, faces all aglow*

—made flower-faces with a smile—

> *Turn, turn from sin and sadness, look up to the sky*

—we frowned on the word *sin* and lifted our faces on the word *sky*—

> *Climb, climb up sunshine mountain, you and I.*

—we pointed to someone else's heart, then to our own.

A hymn or Sunday school song that included hand motions demanded to be performed with no less confidence than a secret clubhouse handshake. Anyone who missed making like a flower, or looking sad when singing *sin*, was demoted to the last rung of the clubhouse ladder and thereby eyed carefully on the next motion-song. One had to keep up.

The hours around the campfire passed too quickly. Mother hadn't piled any driftwood onto the glowing coals for a while, and now the embers merely breathed small ghosts. We closed out the campfire with my father's favorite hymn. It was a hymn of the sea:

> *Brightly beams our Father's mercy*
> *   From his lighthouse evermore;*
> *But to us he gives the keeping*
> *   Of the lights along the shore.*
> *Dark the night of sin has settled,*
> *   Loud the angry billows roar;*

Eager eyes are watching, longing
    For the lights along the shore.
Trim your feeble lamp, my brother!
    Some poor seaman, tempest tossed—
Trying now to make the harbor,
    In the darkness may be lost.
Let the lower lights be burning,
    Send a beam across the waves!
Some poor fainting struggling seaman,
    You may rescue, you may save.

When the ocean mist began to overtake our campfire, we gathered our blankets and trekked back over the dunes to our tents. A flashlight led the way to the top of the barrier dune, between the beach and the smaller sand mounds where our tents nestled. The youngest Eareckson, I trudged behind my father, dragging my blanket.

As we crested the top of the mountainous barrier dune, we paused. To the south I could spot the Fenwick Island lighthouse. To the north, the glow of the town of Rehoboth Beach, miles up the coast. We were high up enough to see the starlight shimmering on Indian River Bay, several hundred yards to the west. The peak of sand we stood on was the only defense between the dark, dangerous ocean and our home continent. I reached for my father's hand.

"Daddy, what does it mean, 'Let the lower lights be burning'?"

My father looked out over the bay. He lifted a hand and pointed straight ahead, into the night. "See those?" he said.

I looked into the dark. A red light on the bay blinked on, then off. A green channel marker did the same.

"Those are the lower lights," he said.

That fact alone amazed me. I was always amazed when some mysterious word or line in a hymn found its counterpart in my world. Seeing a cross on a hill far away. Or coming into a garden alone, where the dew was still on the roses. The first time I ever won a trophy in a Brownies contest, I clutched it tightly and happily, "'til my trophies at last I lay down" on my dresser that night. I was amazed to think heaven might have a judge with trophies to hand out. And here, amazingly, were actual lower lights.

"Lower lights mark where the water is deep enough for a boat to sail safely," Daddy explained. "If those lights go out, sailors won't be able to tell where the sandbar is. Ships have wrecked on many shores for want of channel markers."

"So, why are they called 'lower lights' in the song?"

"God is the lighthouse, and we are his lower lights. We point the way, we show where it's safe to go," he explained. "That's what you do."

"I do?"

He held my hand, and together we slid down the side of the dune.

"Yes, you do," he said. He pronounced it as a fact about me, a fact I knew I was too young to absorb. "It's like what you've learned from the Lord," he said, shifting to a more serious tone, "'Let your light so shine before men.'"

I didn't know much stuff from the Bible. But the way my father said the words made them sound like something King James said, if not the Lord. Or like something Daddy would make up. Whichever, my father expected me to let my light so shine before men. I didn't quite understand what my light was or how I should shine it before men. But that was okay. I could never quite keep straight when things were from the Bible or from my father. This was probably because of the impressive way he shifted his tone of voice, as though he were speaking *ex cathedra*, like a real prophet with a message from heaven. Or it might have been the way he pronounced *Lord* with an Irish brogue. He never did that with any other important word beginning with *L*—only with *Lord*, as if he were Spencer Tracy playing the Irish priest in *Boys Town*. I figured the accent came from my Scots-Irish grandmother, Anna Verona Cacy, whom I never knew. Like Daddy, she was the source of many adventure stories. My father and grandmother had a corner on the *Laard.*

My dad, born John King Eareckson in 1900, should have been born a cabin boy on a clipper ship. He might as well have been. One of his earliest jobs was serving as errand boy for a crew of carpenters and shipbuilders who worked at the Baltimore dry docks, repairing wooden clipper ships. Those men's names were Angus Budreau and Georgy Banks—yes, the same guys who showed up in Daddy's stories—as well as Joe Dowsit and Pete DeVeau, sailing with him out of the Sargasso Sea or prospecting gold in Wind River Canyon. They could handle an adz with the best, and they were rowdy ruffians who drank heartily and cursed loudly. Yet when they tried to entice my father to drink, he refused, as he often told us proudly. He chose instead to go for ice cream made on Pratt Street, near the harbor. Naturally, they dubbed him Ice Cream Johnny. I was convinced my father had made up the rhyme, "I scream, you scream, we all scream for ice cream." I found out otherwise only later, when the Good Humor man told me so.

When Johnny Eareckson became old enough to harness horses, he was up before dawn, hitching the family wagon and making deliveries for his father's coal company. He never completed his schooling, for reasons of which I'm not sure. By the age of nineteen, though, he had started his own flooring company, hurrying to and from jobs on his bicycle. He had to scramble to keep up with his three more-learned brothers: Uncle George, an accountant, Uncle Vince, an architect, and Uncle Milt, a preacher.

John usually came home late to the family's small, brick row house with marble front steps on Stricker Street. He was exhausted every day from heavy labor—a kind of labor different from what his brothers did at their desk, drawing board, or pulpit. There was hardly a night when, creaking open the back door, Johnny didn't encounter his mother, Anna Verona, sitting in the kitchen by the coal stove, an afghan on her lap and a Bible in her hands. She was reading and praying for her boys. Especially for Johnny, the son who didn't fit the mold of his brothers, the one whose heart was a bit more tender and tumultuous, full of passion and adventure. How Anna Eareckson loved her Johnny, she said with an Irish lilt.

And he loved her.

"I'll never forget," he said, shaking his head, "I'd come home from wrestling at the YMCA, my brothers from school and work downtown, and Mother would say to us, 'We need coal for the stove tonight. Vince, it's your turn.' My brothers and I would be clowning around by the sink, snapping towels at each other, and Vince would say that it was George's turn. 'Not mine, it's Milton's,' and Milt would point at me, and I would push Vince and . . . before you knew it, there we'd see Mother, smudged with black dust, trudging up the cellar steps in her long skirts, carrying a heavy bucket of coal in her frail hands. It about busted my heart open."

My father's mother died young. She worked herself into an early grave. It was something Daddy never seemed able to forgive himself for, as if a family of four strapping, healthy boys could have—*should* have—somehow eased their mother's labor. It explained why, whenever my father spoke her maiden name, *Anna Verona Cacy*, he did so with such fondness of heart and with that Irish lilt. It also told me why he loved to sing "Let the Lower Lights Be Burning," one of my grandmother's favorite hymns.

> *Let the lower lights be burning,*
> *Send a beam across the waves!*
> *Some poor fainting, struggling seaman*
> *You may rescue, you may save.*

When Daddy and I got back to camp, we plopped our things down by the picnic table. Uncle George was closing up the Coleman stove. He had fried his prized soft-shell crabs for dinner that evening. Nearby, aglow with the light from the hissing propane lantern, my mother and a few aunts were putting things away in the coolers. Taking the lantern in hand, Mommy led my sisters and me to the little pup-tent beyond our camp, which served as our makeshift latrine. From there, she lit the way back to our huge army tent and through the wooden screen door. We slid off our sandy shorts and donned sweatshirts over our damp underwear. That's what I liked about camping at the beach—we could sleep in something fun beside pajamas.

Brushing the sand off our feet, we ducked under the mosquito netting and climbed into our cots. My cot was in the corner, and I loved it when the weather was pleasant enough to keep the tent's sides rolled up. That way, I could hear the adults whispering and the hissing of the lantern. As a night breeze flapped the netting, I would nestle into my pillow, clutch my stuffed rabbit, and fight off sleep as long as I could. I wanted to savor the taste of salt air, the aroma of coffee being prepared for tomorrow's breakfast, the hushed conversation of my mother, father, and relatives, and the cotton down of my warm sleeping bag. I knew no mosquito buzzing overhead could invade. Under the protective netting, I was safe. As safe as under the covers in my own bedroom, gazing at my favorite bedside plaque, the one of the little girl in her boat.

> *Dear God, my little boat and I*
> *are on your open sea.*
> *Please guide us safely through the waves*
> *my little boat and me.*

I wondered what adventures tomorrow would bring. I hoped I would be wakened by the smell of sizzling bacon. Maybe Daddy would make his poached eggs—an egg fried in a hot skillet, a cup full of water splashed in at the last minute, a lid to cover, and salt and pepper to season. I hoped Uncle George had put the ice from Lewis Dairy into the big milk jug, so the water would taste icy-cold from the dipper. I wondered if my cousin Little Eddie and my sister Kathy and I would discover any horseshoe crabs or conch shells in the tide pools. Or if we would play horse, galloping up and down the sand hills that stretched for miles on either side of our tent. I hoped the day would be bright and hot, so that when

I lay on the sand with my cheek against my forearm, I would smell the sweet Coppertone.

I hoped we would make castles in the sand with Aunt Lee and Uncle Eddie, dig after burrowing sand crabs, watch the waves erase our footprints, shower when the sun went down, and slather Noxzema on our sun-pinkened skin. In the evening, after crab cakes, we'd help Mom wash the pots and pans in the ocean. Then we would drive to Rehoboth Beach, to walk the boardwalk and have ice cream or hot french fries with vinegar. Most of all, I hoped we would enjoy another fire on the beach. And another story from Daddy. Or Uncle George singing "Ramona," while holding up his cigar and leading us all like an impresario.

Whatever I hoped, I would not be disappointed. The flapping of the mosquito netting hypnotized us into sleep. "Goodnight, girls," I heard Daddy whisper. Or maybe—*I hoped*—it was God.

I don't know if they make many fathers like the one who raised me. No, I don't think so. How many daddies saw the Wright Brothers plane fly over Baltimore, or one of the first Model-T Fords chug down Howard Street? How many dads weave their children into a whole world of adventure, through the tales they spin by heart? My father traded with Indians in British Columbia and fought bears near the Yukon border—yes, I'm sure he did fight that bear with his hands, and that it wasn't just a story. Really. But even if the one about the bear didn't happen, I knew my father's tender heart and fine character and love for the Laard were real.

The next evening, just as I'd hoped, we returned to camp from Rehoboth Beach early enough for a fire. Soon the driftwood that my sisters Linda, Jay, Kathy, and I had collected during the day was roaring, and the stars were sprinkled above us from one horizon to the other, like vast powdered sugar. The curling of the waves glowed phosphorescent from the red tide, and my Uncle Eddie had just finished singing "You Are My Sunshine."

"Do your poem, Daddy," I chimed, "the one about the bar."

Ever the literalist, I had only recently discovered that this, my father's classic recitation, wasn't about a saloon.

Daddy stuck his hands in the pockets of his baggy pants and stared at the fire. Then he began his litany, which was more Eareckson than Tennyson. The poem came from somewhere deep down in my father's breast. As he spoke its haunting lines, I wanted badly for someone to please reach up and hold onto him, lest he turn toward the waves and cross the bar without me.

> *Sunset and evening star,*
> *And one clear call for me,*
> *And may there be no moaning of the bar,*
> *When I put out to sea.*
> *But such a tide as moving seems asleep,*
> *Too full for sound and foam,*
> *When that which drew from out the boundless deep*
> *Turns again home.*
> *Twilight and evening bell,*
> *And after that the dark!*
> *And may there be no sadness of farewell,*
> *When I embark;*
> *For tho' from out our bourne of time and place*
> *The flood may bear me far,*
> *I hope to see my Pilot face to face*
> *When I have crossed the bar.*

No one ever broke the silence that followed one of my father's poems. We simply kept listening while the lines settled in, the way you'd listen to a retreating sheet of surf before the next heavy wave crashed down. I didn't understand the poem, except for the part about seeing the Pilot—I surmised that was God. But my heart nearly twisted in half to think that my father loved a poem about dying.

I remember reaching for Kathy's hand. I knew she would understand my fear. We shared a bed together back home. Often, after

Daddy finished telling a bedtime story, and we heard him walk down the stairs, we lay in the dark listening to our breathing. I reached for her hand once then and murmured, "What if something awful happens?"—I wanted to add "to Daddy" but couldn't choke out the words.

"I know what you mean," my sister whispered back. "I know what you mean about Dad." She held my hand then, and she held it now too, in the dancing shadows formed by the fire.

Daddy closed the poem with the same beautiful hymn we'd sung the night before. My sisters and I crescendoed on the line,

> *Some poor fainting, struggling seaman,*
> *You may rescue, you may save.*

Once again, all felt safe.

Surely my father rescued poor, fainting, struggling seamen. If not on the Sargasso Sea, then for certain during his merchant marine days. Yet never did I dream then that, in the not-too-distant future, I would be the poor, struggling, fainting one, going down for the third time, drowning in waves of grief higher than any surf. More terrifying than any Dutchman's curse.

And even Daddy wouldn't be able to help.

THE CASE

FOR A

CREATOR

A Journalist Investigates New
Scientific Evidence That Points Toward God

LEE STROBEL

Author of *The Case for Christ* and *The Case for Faith*

My road to atheism was paved by science—but, ironically, so was my later journey to God.

Like many students, I studied scientific discoveries that seemed to put God out of a job. I learned about experiments that suggested life was created solely through natural processes. Charles Darwin's theory appeared to account for how life became increasingly complex through the eons. Soon I placed my faith in the hard facts of science, convinced that they made the idea of a supernatural deity unnecessary.

However, my wife's conversion to Christianity and the incredible changes in her life prompted me to begin considering whether God might actually exist. My book *The Case for Christ* describes the historical evidence that led me to conclude Jesus really is the unique Son of God. In *The Case for Faith*, I probed the eight toughest objections that stood between me and God, finding satisfying answers to each of them.

My newest book, *The Case for a Creator*, retraces my investigation into scientific evidence for God. To my amazement, I learned that when science is applied appropriately, it actually supports the idea of a Designer who made us in his image. Using an interview format that helps make the issues easy to understand, my book explores the latest evidence from cosmology, physics, astronomy, microbiology, genetics, and cognitive science, and demonstrates how the evidence points persuasively toward a Creator.

If your belief in God has been undermined by science, or if you want to help a friend or family member who's struggling in this area, then join me on this fascinating journey of discovery. Ultimately, you'll find as I did that science can be a powerful ally of faith.

Lee Strobel

THE CASE FOR A CREATOR

The deadline was looming for the Green Streak, the afternoon edition of the *Chicago Tribune*, and the frenzied atmosphere in the newsroom was carbonated with activity. Teletypes clattered behind Plexiglas partitions. Copy boys darted from desk to desk. Reporters hunched over their typewriters in intense concentration. Editors barked into telephones. On the wall, a huge clock counted down the minutes.

A copy boy hustled into the cavernous room and tossed three copies of the *Chicago Daily News*, hot off the presses, onto the middle of the city desk. Assistant city editors lunged at them and hungrily scanned the front page to see if the competition had beaten them on anything. One of them let out a grunt. In one motion, he ripped out an article and then pivoted, waving it in the face of a reporter who had made the mistake of hovering too closely.

"Recover this!" he demanded. Without looking at it, the reporter grabbed the scrap and headed for his desk to quickly make some phone calls and produce a similar story so it wouldn't look like the *Trib* had been scooped.

Reporters at City Hall, the Criminal Courts Building, the State of Illinois Building, and police headquarters were phoning assistant city editors to "dope" their stories. Once the reporters had provided a quick capsule of the situation, the assistants would cover their phone with a hand and ask their boss, the city editor, for a decision on how the article should be handled.

"The cops were chasing a car and it hit a bus," one of them called over to the city editor. "Five injured, none seriously."

"School bus?"

"City bus."

The city editor frowned. "Gimme a four-head," came the order—code for a three-paragraph story.

"Four-head," the assistant repeated into the phone. He pushed a button to connect the reporter to a rewrite man, who would take down details on a typewriter and then craft the item in a matter of minutes.

The year was 1974. I was a rookie, just three months out of the University of Missouri's Journalism School. I had worked on smaller newspapers since I was fourteen, but this was the big leagues. I was already addicted to the adrenaline.

On that particular day, though, I felt more like a spectator than a participant. I strolled over to the city desk and unceremoniously dropped my story into the "in" basket. It was a meager offering— a one-paragraph "brief" about two pipe bombs exploding in the south suburbs. The item was destined for section three, page ten, in a journalistic trash heap called "metropolitan briefs." My fortunes, however, were about to change.

Standing outside his glass-walled office, the assistant managing editor caught my attention. "C'mere," he called.

I walked over. "What's up?"

"Look at this," he said as he handed me a piece of wire copy. He didn't wait for me to read it before he started filling me in.

"Crazy stuff in West Virginia," he said. "People getting shot, schools getting bombed—all because some hillbillies are mad about the textbooks being used in the schools."

"You're kidding," I said. "Good story."

My eyes scanned the brief Associated Press report. I quickly noticed that pastors were denouncing textbooks as being "anti-God" and that rallies were being held in churches. My stereotypes clicked in.

"Christians, huh?" I said. "So much for loving their neighbors. And not being judgmental."

He motioned for me to follow him over to a safe along the wall. He twirled the dial and opened it, reaching in to grab two packets of twenty dollar bills.

"Get out to West Virginia and check it out," he said as he handed me the six hundred dollars of expense money. "Give me a story for the Bulldog." He was referring to the first edition of next Sunday's paper. That didn't give me much time. It was already noon on Monday.

I started to walk away, but the editor grabbed my arm. "Look—be careful," he said.

I was oblivious. "What do you mean?"

He gestured toward the AP story I was clutching. "These hillbillies hate reporters," he said. "They've already beaten up two of them. Things are volatile. Be smart."

I couldn't tell if the surge I felt was fear or exhilaration. In the end it didn't really matter. I knew I had to do whatever it would take to get the story. But the irony wasn't lost on me: these people were followers of the so-called Prince of Peace, and yet I was being warned to keep on guard to avoid getting roughed up.

"*Christians . . . ,*" I muttered under my breath. Hadn't they heard, as one skeptic famously put it, that modern science had already dissolved Christianity in a vat of nitric acid?

IS DARWIN RESPONSIBLE?

From the gleaming office buildings in downtown Charleston to the dreary backwood hamlets in surrounding Kanawha County, the situation was tense when I arrived the next day and began poking around for a story. Many parents were keeping their kids out of school; coal miners had walked off the job in wildcat strikes, threatening to cripple the local economy; school buses were being shot at; firebombs had been lobbed at some empty classrooms; picketers were marching with signs saying, "Even Hillbillies Have Constitutional Rights." Violence had left two people seriously injured. Intimidation and threats were rampant.

The wire services could handle the day-to-day breaking developments in the crisis; I planned to write an overview article that explained the dynamics of the controversy. Working from my hotel room, I called for appointments with key figures in the conflict and then drove in my rental car from homes to restaurants to schools to offices in order to interview them. I quickly found that just mentioning the word *textbook* to anybody in these parts would instantly release a flood of vehement opinion as thick as the lush trees that carpet the Appalachian hillsides.

"The books bought for our school children would teach them to lose their love of God, to honor draft dodgers and revolutionaries, and to lose their respect for their parents," insisted the intense, dark-haired wife of a Baptist minister as I interviewed her on the front porch of her house. As a recently elected school-board member, she was leading the charge against the textbooks.

A community activist was just as opinionated in the other direction. "For the first time," she told me, "these textbooks reflect real Americanism, and I think it's exciting. Americanism, to me, is listening to all kinds of voices, not just white Anglo-Saxon Protestants."

The school superintendent, who had resigned at the height of the controversy, only shook his head in disdain when I asked him what he thought. "People around here are going flaky," he sighed. "Both poles are wrong."

Meanwhile, ninety-six thousand copies of three hundred different textbooks had been temporarily removed from classrooms and stored in cardboard cartons at a warehouse west of Charleston. They included Scott Foresman Co.'s Galaxy series, McDougal, Little Co.'s Man series, Allyn & Bacon Inc.'s Breakthrough series, and such classics as *The Lord of the Flies, Of Human Bondage, Moby Dick, The Old Man and the Sea, Animal Farm*, and Plato's *Republic*.

What were people so angry about? Some said they were outraged at the situational ethics propounded in some of the books. One textbook included the story of a child cheating a merchant out of a penny. Students were asked: "Most people think that cheating is wrong. Do you think there is ever a time when it might be right? Tell when it is. Tell why you think it is right." Parents seized on this as undermining the Christian values they were attempting to inculcate into their children.

"We're trying to get our kids to do the right thing," the parent of an elementary school student told me in obvious frustration. "Then these books come along and say that sometimes the wrong thing is the right thing. We just don't believe in that! The Ten Commandments are the Ten Commandments."

But there was also an undercurrent of something else: an inchoate fear of the future, of change, of new ideas, of cultural transformation. I could sense a simmering frustration in people over how modernity was eroding the foundation of their faith. "Many of the protesters," wrote the *Charleston Gazette*, "are demonstrating against a changing world."

This underlying concern was crystallized for me in a conversation with a local businessman over hamburgers at a Charleston diner. When I asked him why he was so enraged over the textbooks, he reached into his pocket and took out a newspaper clipping about the textbook imbroglio.

"Listen to what *Dynamics of Language* tells our kids," he said as he quoted an excerpt from the textbook: "'Read the theory of divine origin and the story of the Tower of Babel as told in Genesis. Be prepared to explain one or more ways these stories could be interpreted.'"

He tossed the well-worn clipping on the table in disgust. "The *theory* of divine origin!" he declared. "The Word of God is *not* a theory. Take God out of creation and what's left? Evolution? Scientists want to teach our kids that divine origin is just a theory that stupid people believe, but that evolution is a scientific fact. Well, it's not. And that's at the bottom of this."

I cocked my head. "Are you saying Charles Darwin is responsible for all of this?"

"Let me put it this way," he said. "If Darwin's right, we're just sophisticated monkeys. The Bible is wrong. There is no God. And without God, there's no right or wrong. We can just make up our morals as we go. The basis for all we believe is destroyed. And that's why this country is headed to hell in a hand basket. Is Darwin responsible? I'll say this: people have to choose between science and faith, between evolution and the Bible, between the Ten Commandments and make-'em-up-as-you-go ethics. We've made our choice—and we're not budging."

He took a swig of beer. "Have you seen the teacher's manual?" he asked. I shook my head. "It says students should compare the Bible story of Daniel in the Lion's Den to that myth about a lion. You know which one I'm talking about?"

"Androcles and the Lion?" I asked, referring to the Aesop fable about an escaped slave who removed a thorn from the paw of a lion he encountered in the woods. Later, the recaptured slave was to be eaten by a lion for the entertainment of the crowd at the Roman Coliseum, but it turned out to be the same lion he had befriended. Instead of eating him, the lion gently licked his hand, which impressed the emperor so much that the slave was set free.

"Yeah, that's the one," the businessman said as he wagged a French fry at me. "What does it tell our kids when they're supposed to compare that to the Bible? That the Bible is just a bunch of fairy tales? That it's all a myth? That you can interpret the Bible any way you darn well please, even if it rips the guts out of what it really says? We've got to put our foot down. I'm not going to let a bunch of eggheads destroy the faith of my children."

I felt like I was finally getting down to the root of the controversy. I scribbled down his words as best I could. Part of me, though, wanted to debate him. Didn't he know that evolution *is* a proven fact? Didn't he realize that in an age of science and technology that it's simply irrational to believe the ancient myths about God creating the world and shaping human beings in his own image? Did he really want his children clinging desperately to religious pap that is so clearly disproved by modern cosmology, astronomy, zoology, comparative anatomy, geology, paleontology, biology, genetics, and anthropology? I was tempted to say, "Hey, what *is* the difference between Daniel in the Lion's Den and Androcles and the Lion? They're *both* fairy tales!"

But I wasn't there to get into an argument. I was there to report the story. And what a bizarre story it was! In the last part of the twentieth century, in an era when we had split the atom and landed people on the moon and found fossils to prove evolution beyond all doubt, a bunch of religious zealots were tying a county into knots because they just can't let go of religious folklore that simply defies all reason.

I thought for a moment. "One more question," I said. "Do you ever have any doubts?"

He waved his hand as if to draw my attention to the universe. "Look at the world," he said. "God's fingerprints are all over it. I'm absolutely sure of that. How else do you explain nature and human beings? And God has told us how to live. If we ignore him—well, then the whole world's in for a whole lot of trouble."

I reached for the check. "Thanks for your opinions," I told him.

STANDING TRIAL IN WEST VIRGINIA

All of this was good stuff for my story, but I needed more. The leaders I had interviewed had all denounced the violence as being the unfortunate actions of a few hotheads. But to tell the whole story, I needed to see the underbelly of the controversy. I wanted to tap into the rage of those who chose violence over debate. My opportunity quickly came.

A rally, I heard, was being planned for Friday night over in the isolated, heavily wooded community of Campbell's Creek. The more militant parents were expected to gather and vote on whether to continue to keep their kids out of school. Tempers were at a boiling point. And the word was that reporters were not welcome. It seemed that folks were incensed over the way some big newspapers had caricatured them as know-nothing hillbillies, so this was to be a private gathering of the faithful. They could really speak their mind if no journalists were present.

This was my chance. I decided to infiltrate the rally in order to get an unvarnished look at what was really going on. At the time, it seemed like a good idea.

I rendezvoused with Charlie, a top-notch photojournalist dispatched by the *Tribune* to capture the textbook war on film. We decided together that we would sneak into the rural school where hundreds of agitated protestors were expected to pack the bleachers. I'd scribble my notes surreptitiously; Charlie would see whether he could snap a few discreet photos. We figured if we could just blend into the crowd, we'd get away with it.

We figured wrong.

Our shiny new rental car contrasted with the dusty pick-up trucks and well-used cars that were left at all angles on the gravel parking lot. We tried to be as inconspicuous as possible as we walked nonchalantly alongside the stragglers who were streaming toward the gymnasium. Charlie kept his Nikons hidden underneath his waist-length denim jacket, but there was no way he could conceal his long black hair.

At first, I thought we had gotten away with it. We flowed with the crowd through a side door of the gym. Inside, the noise was deafening. Two large bleachers were packed with animated and agitated people who all seemed to be talking at once. Someone was setting up a small speaker on the floor of the gym. Charlie and I were milling around with people who were standing by the door, unable to find a seat. Nobody seemed to be paying any attention to us.

A beefy man in a white short-sleeve shirt and dark, narrow tie took the handheld microphone and blew into it to see if it was working. "Let me have your attention," he shouted over the din. "Let's get started."

People began to settle down. But as they did, I got the uncomfortable feeling that a lot of eyes were starting to bore in on us. "Wait a minute," the guy at the microphone said. "We've got some intruders here!" With that, he turned and glared at Charlie and me. People around us pivoted to confront the two of us. The room fell silent.

"C'mon out here!" the man demanded, gesturing for both of us to come onto the gym floor. "Who are you? You're not welcome here!"

With that, the crowd erupted into catcalls and jeers. Unsure what to do, Charlie and I stepped hesitantly toward the man with the microphone. It seemed like all of the anger in the room was suddenly focused on the two of us. My first thought was that I didn't like becoming part of the story. My second thought was that this mob was going to throw us out of the place—and we were going to get roughed up along the way. My third thought was that nothing in journalism school had prepared me for this.

"What should we do with these two boys?" the man asked, baiting the crowd. Now the folks were really riled! I felt like I was being put on trial. I used to hear the phrase, "my knees were shaking," and think it was just a figure of speech. But my knees *were* shaking!

"Let's get rid of them!" he declared.

The door was blocked. There was nowhere to run. But just as some men were surging forward to grab us, a part-time truck driver, part-time preacher stepped up and wrested away the microphone. He raised his hand to stop them.

"Hold on!" he shouted. "Just a minute! Settle down!" Obviously, he was someone the crowd respected. The noise subsided. "Now listen to me," he continued. "I've seen this reporter around town the last several days, interviewing both sides of this thing. I think he wants to tell the story like it is. I think he wants to be fair. I say we give him a chance. I say we let him stay!"

The crowd was uncertain. There was some grumbling. The preacher turned toward me. "You're gonna be fair, aren't you?" he asked.

I nodded as reassuringly as I could.

The preacher turned to the crowd. "How else are we going to get our story out?" he asked. "Let's welcome these fellas and trust they're gonna do the right thing!"

That seemed to convince them. The mood quickly shifted. In fact, some people started applauding. Instead of throwing us out, someone ushered us to seats in the front row of the bleachers.

Charlie took out his cameras and began snapping pictures. I took out my notebook and pen.

"WE'LL WIN—ONE WAY OR THE OTHER"

The preacher took control of the meeting. He turned to the crowd and held aloft a book titled *Facts About V.D.* "This is gonna turn your stomachs, but this is the kind of book your children are reading!" he shouted in his Andy Griffith accent.

There were gasps. "Get those books out of the schools!" someone shouted. "Get 'em out!" several others echoed as if they were saying "amen" at a revival meeting.

The preacher began to pace back and forth, perspiration rings expanding on his white shirt as he waved the book. "Y'all have got to force yourselves to look at these books so you can really understand what the issue is all about!" he declared. "Your children may be reading these books. This is not the way to teach our kids about sex—divorced from morality, divorced from God. And that's why we've got to continue keeping our kids out of school for another week to boycott these filthy, un-American, anti-religious books."

That catapulted the crowd into a clapping frenzy. Money poured into the Kentucky Fried Chicken buckets being passed around for donations to fight the textbook battle.

The rally continued in that vein for another half hour or so. At one point, the preacher's words were reminiscent of the businessman's comments earlier in the week. "We're not evolved from slime," he declared defiantly. "We're created in the image of God Almighty. And he's given us the best textbook in the world to tell us how to live!" The folks roared their approval.

"The only victory we'll accept is a total victory," he declared. "We'll win—one way or the other."

When he raised the issue of whether the school boycott should be continued through the coming week, the resounding response was yes. The goal of the rally accomplished, he issued a quick "God bless y'all," and the meeting was over.

Now I had all the color I needed for my story. I hustled back to my hotel and banged out a piece for Sunday's paper, which appeared on the front page under the headline "Textbook Battle

Rages in Bible Belt County." I followed that with an in-depth article that also ran on the front page the next day.

Settling back into my seat as I flew back to Chicago, I reflected on the experience and concluded that I had fulfilled my promise to the preacher: I had been fair to both sides. My articles were balanced and responsible. But, frankly, it had been difficult.

Inside that gymnasium Friday night, I felt like I had stared Christianity in the face—and saw it for the dinosaur it was. Why couldn't these people get their heads out of the sand and admit the obvious: science had put their God out of a job! White-coated scientists of the modern world had trumped the black-robed priests of medieval times. Darwin's theory of evolution—no, the absolute *fact* of evolution—meant that there is no universal morality decreed by a deity, only culturally conditioned values that vary from place to place and situation to situation.

I knew intuitively what prominent evolutionary scientist William Provine of Cornell University would spell out explicitly in a debate years later. If Darwinism is true, he said, then there are five inescapable conclusions: there's no evidence for God; there's no life after death; there's no absolute foundation for right and wrong; there's no ultimate meaning for life; and people don't really have free will.

To me, the controversy in West Virginia was a symbolic last gasp of an archaic belief system hurtling toward oblivion. As more and more young people were taught the iron-clad evidence for evolution, as they understood the impossibility of miracles, as they saw how science was on the path to ultimately explaining everything in the universe, then belief in an invisible God, in angels and demons, in a long-ago rabbi who walked on water and multiplied fish and bread and returned from the dead, would fade into a fringe superstition confined only to dreary backwoods hamlets like Campbell's Creek, West Virginia.

As far as I was concerned, that day couldn't come soon enough.

If I had stopped asking questions, that's where my opinions would have remained. But with my background in journalism and law, asking questions was woven into my nature. And when my wife, Leslie, announced several years later that after a period of spiritual seeking she had decided to become a follower of Jesus, the first words I uttered were in the form of a question.

It wasn't asked politely. Instead, it was spewed in an angry and accusatory tone: *"What has gotten into you?"* I simply couldn't understand how such a rational person could buy into an irrational, anti-scientific concoction of wishful thinking, make believe, mythology, and legend.

In the ensuing months, however, as her character began to change, as her values underwent a transformation, as she became a more loving and caring and authentic person, I began asking the same question, only this time in a soft and sincere tone of genuine wonderment: *"What has gotten into you?"* Something—or, as she would claim, Someone—was undeniably changing her for the better.

Clearly, I needed to investigate what was going on. And so I began asking more questions—a lot of them—about faith, God, and the Bible. I was determined to go wherever the answers would take me—even though, frankly, I wasn't quite prepared back then for where I would ultimately end up.

This multifaceted spiritual investigation lasted nearly two years. In one of my previous books, *The Case for Christ*, which retraced this journey, I discussed the answers I received from thirteen leading experts about the historical evidence for Jesus of Nazareth. Today I stand absolutely convinced that despite the outdated critiques of liberal theologians, the most reliable historical facts point convincingly toward Jesus Christ as being the unique Son of God who confirmed his divine identity by rising from the dead.

In the subsequent book, *The Case for Faith*, I pursued answers to the "Big Eight" questions about Christianity—the kind of issues that began troubling me even as a youngster but which nobody had been willing to answer. I confirmed that there are compelling and satisfying explanations for such thorny issues as why there's pain and suffering in the world and whether contemporary people can really believe in the miraculous.

But there was another important dimension to my investigation that I barely touched upon in those earlier books. Because science had played such an instrumental role in propelling me toward atheism, I devoted a lot of time to posing questions about what the latest research says about God. With an open mind, I began asking experts:

- Are science and faith doomed to always be at war? Was I right to think that a science-minded individual must necessarily eschew religious beliefs? Or is there a fundamentally different way to view the relationship between the spiritual and the scientific?
- Has the scientific evidence of the last fifty years—in cosmology, astronomy, biochemistry, cognitive sciences, physics, and so forth—tended to point toward or away from the existence of God?
- Is the information I was taught in school about evolution still valid in light of the most recent scientific discoveries?

"Science," said two-time Nobel Prize winner Linus Pauling, "is the search for the truth." Seeking the truth means setting aside preconceptions and being willing to reconsider personal convictions if the evidence warrants it. It means cross-examining experts who are willing to challenge the scientific status quo if the data are leading elsewhere. It means actively engaging in a thorough investigation.

So join me as I pack my suitcase and travel around the country—from California to Georgia to Pennsylvania and beyond—to retrace and expand upon my original investigation of the scientific evidence for God. In posing the questions that plagued me as a skeptic, perhaps I'll be asking the very questions that have proven to be sticking points in your own spiritual journey.

But be ready. Be prepared to be amazed—even dazzled—by what scientists are unearthing. Be willing to challenge what you may have been taught in a classroom long ago. Most of all, resolve right now to go wherever the evidence leads.

Scientists will tell you that this is entirely appropriate. "All scientific knowledge," says no less an authority than the National Academy of Sciences, "is, in principle, subject to change as new evidence becomes available."

THE SECRET OF RECEIVING WHAT YOU NEED FROM GOD

BREAK THROUGH
Prayer

JIM CYMBALA

AUTHOR OF THE BEST-SELLING *FRESH WIND, FRESH FIRE*

*S*ince I've never had the opportunity of attending seminary, God has regularly used theological books to give me much-needed instruction. Of the more than two thousand volumes that line the shelves of my study, none have meant more to me than books on the subject of prayer. They have proven invaluable to my own spiritual growth because they have driven me both to the Scriptures and to my knees.

When I reach heaven, I will want to meet and thank the saints who wrote the books that so affected my life. People like David Brainerd, E. M. Bounds, Charles Finney, and Samuel Chadwick have an investment in my life although they lived decades and centuries ago. They and others did much more than lay out the principles of prayer. Their writings ignited my faith and inspired me to call on the name of the Lord. Countless breakthroughs in my life and ministry can be traced to God's using their writings to help this needy pastor in New York City.

Breakthrough Prayer is aimed at more than outlining the important biblical principle of seeking God's help. It is also about what I call the lost prayers of Scripture—the things we rarely pray for even though God has promised them to all his children. For example, when was the last time you heard others pray for joy or to understand God's timing for their lives? We individuals and our churches all suffer great loss when we fail to ask God for the blessings he wants to give us. The following chapters are written in hopes that no one who reads this book will suffer the tragedy of a life summed up by these words from Scripture: "You do not have, because you do not ask God" (James 4:2).

During my pilgrimage of prayer I have also come across a host of books that "clinically" analyze the subject but fail to draw the heart toward the throne of grace. Although biblically correct in their doctrine, they have fallen short of their purpose. Many also fail to highlight the main pitfalls that most often hinder a spirit of prayer in us. Effective praying depends not just on "what to do," but also on "what never to do" if we want answers from God. By his grace, I pray that this book will instruct, inspire, and assist many in breaking through to a new life of asking and receiving from God.

Jim Cymbala

BREAK THROUGH *Blessings*

It was a sweltering night in New York. My wife, Carol, and I along with a handful of others had gathered around the altar of our little church in Brooklyn. As we stood together in that rundown building, tears flowing freely and our voices lifted in prayer, we knew that our struggling church faced problems only God could defeat. If anything was going to change, if the church was ever going to reach its potential, one critical ingredient was absolutely required. We could not live one more day without breaking through to the blessing of God.

But what exactly was this blessing we sought? As the young pastor of that inner-city church, I was beginning to realize that the blessing of God is something very real and tangible. It can change a man's life, transform a neighborhood, invigorate a church, and even alter the course of history. Often it is given to the most unlikely people, like a friend of mine whose life seemed cursed from the start. He is a great example of the difference God can make.

Perched on a hill high above the village of Las Piedras was a house dedicated to the powers of darkness. Inside lived a family that earned its living through practicing sorcery, holding séances, and trafficking with evil spirits. The father, a large man who was feared throughout Puerto Rico, was known as "the Great One." His wife assisted in the work and bore him eighteen children—seventeen sons and a lone daughter. The house on the hill became a favorite lodging place for mediums and spiritualists throughout the island.

One of the children was especially affected by growing up in that house. Though he got into trouble early and often, he feared the sorcery practiced there and resented the lack of attention he felt as one among so many children. One day his father caught him stealing from his mother's purse. As punishment, the five-year-old was locked into a filthy little pigeon house. The boy tried frantically to escape but only succeeded in exciting the birds who slammed into his little body as they flew around in the darkness. After his father released him, the boy cried hysterically for several hours. The ordeal caused him repeated nightmares.

This son, out of all the others, seemed marked for evil. When he was only eight years old, his mother proclaimed that he was not her son but a "son of Satan, a child of the devil!" When he yelled back in anger, "I hate you!" she merely laughed in his face. He was a cursed child in a house of curses.

The boy grew quickly into an uncontrollable rebel. He tried running away from home on five occasions, and the hatred he felt for his parents turned into contempt for all authority. Unable to deal with their troubled son, his parents sent him to New York City at the age of fifteen. Upon arriving at the airport, he quickly disappeared into the streets for two days. Relatives there eventually enrolled him in school, but he was expelled after repeatedly threatening students, teachers, and the school's principal. Soon after that, he left his relatives' home and took up living on the street in one of the toughest neighborhoods in the city.

The young man's life continued to cycle downward. What else could happen to a kid who had been cursed by his own mother, abused by a father who was a satanic priest, and dedicated to the devil?

Nicky Cruz soon became the warlord of a vicious street gang called the Mau Maus. The smoldering rage inside him found expression in violence, crime, and bloodshed. He was a twisted psychopath who frightened even his friends. (A police psychiatrist told him after an evaluation that he was on a fast track to the electric chair.)

Then one day God sent a street preacher who dared to proclaim the gospel of Jesus Christ to him. Incredibly, the gang leader surrendered his life to Christ. The change was instantaneous. Instead of being full of tortured, self-destructive rage, the young man became filled with love and compassion for hopeless cases—kids like him who seemed bent on destroying themselves.

Before long, Nicky began attending a Bible school in California, where he met his future wife. Later, Nicky returned to Puerto Rico and witnessed the conversion of both his parents. Over time, the Lord opened doors all over the world for him to share his story, and he became one of the greatest evangelists of his generation. Untold thousands of people have been led to Christ by this man once dedicated to the devil. Today his four daughters and their husbands and children are all serving the Lord.

The curse on Nicky Cruz was real, but God's blessing canceled the curse.[1]

Unlike Nicky, Carol and I had been believers since childhood, but we were still desperate for God's blessing. Our breakthrough began in that sticky, uncomfortable, old church during a Tuesday night when a handful of believers were crying out in prayer. The Lord would indeed bless us beyond our wildest imagination, using us to reach out to thousands of broken people—drug addicts, drunks, homeless people, and criminals as well as many professional people who also desperately needed to experience God's blessing. Surprises were coming straight from God in heaven, and the surprises continue to this day.

BLESSING THE PEOPLE

Although God has richly blessed us over the years in some dramatic ways, I'm convinced that the kinds of blessings we enjoy are intended for every church and every believer who earnestly prays for them.

Let's look at what the Bible has to say about God's blessing. First of all, it's important to note that God's blessing is a reflection of his incredible love for his creation. While it is invisible in its essence, his blessing is invincible, overcoming everything that earth or hell can throw against it. This blessing is rooted in the ancient instructions God gave to Moses to be carried out by the high priest of Israel:

> The LORD said to Moses, "Tell Aaron and his sons, 'This is how you are to bless the Israelites. Say to them: "The LORD *bless* you and keep you; the LORD make his face shine upon you and be gracious to you; the LORD turn his face toward you and give you peace."' So they will put my name on the Israelites, and *I will bless them*" (Numbers 6:22–27).

This practice of conferring a priestly blessing in the name of the Lord is what separated Israel from the people around them for all the centuries of its history. Only God's covenant people enjoyed the divine blessing. A nation favored and protected by the Lord, they knew that God had promised to listen to their prayers and be attentive to their problems. The God of the universe had turned his face toward them so that they could receive his supernatural grace. What a privilege to live under the Lord's favor, to daily experience his blessing! What enemy could intimidate them when God was with them in power?

The good news is that God is still a blessing God. In fact, the Bible could be characterized as a book revealing the Lord's intense desire to bless the men and women who belong to him.

If this surprises you, you have only to consider the fact that love *always* desires to bless the object of its affection. I'm reminded of this every Christmas Eve as our family gathers to celebrate. Whenever we get together, I'm not thinking about what gifts I might receive. Like most parents and grandparents, that's the last thing on my mind. Instead, I'm thinking about my children and grandchildren, watching as they open the gift-wrapped boxes Carol and I have prepared for them. My joy comes from giving, not from receiving.

Ask yourself whom you most enjoy giving to. That will tell you whom you really love. Self-centered folks find their greatest delight in spending money on themselves, but when you love someone else, your heart is always going out to bless and help them.

This explains why the Hebrew word *barak* and its derivatives are used more than 330 times in the Old Testament. It's the word for "bless" or "blessing," a word first mentioned in Genesis 1:22 regarding the creatures of the sea: "God blessed them and said, 'Be fruitful and increase in number and fill the water in the seas.'" If God desired to bless crabs and tuna, just think of his interest in helping you and me, creatures who are made in his image! In fact, the very first words recorded after the Lord created Adam and Eve are these: "God *blessed* them" (Genesis 1:28).

God's blessing was the secret behind Noah's escape from the flood. Scripture tells us that "God *blessed* Noah and his sons" (Genesis 9:1). The divine blessing also enabled them to face the daunting task of leaving their ark of safety and starting over. God blessed them first of all by delivering them from judgment and then by providing for them and making them fruitful as they built a new life together.

Like Noah, what stands out about every man and woman God uses for his glory is that they have the special favor of heaven resting upon them. The best words any of us could ever hope to hear from God are the same ones he spoke to Abraham: "I will make you into a great nation [that is, something beyond yourself] and I will bless you" (Genesis 12:2). There it is in its simplest form. God wanted to change Abraham into a great nation, and he wants to change each of us into something more wonderful than we are at present, showering us with his blessings. How could perfect Love ever want anything less for those for whom he gave his Son as a sacrifice for sin?

> God wants to change each of us into something more wonderful than we are at present, showering us with his blessings.

God doesn't want us merely to enjoy a moderate amount of blessings. He wants to bless us abundantly. How else could the rest of his word to our father Abraham be fulfilled: "and *you will be* a blessing" (Genesis 12:2)? Like Abraham, we bless others when God's favor overflows in our lives so much that it affects the world around us. When that happens, the Lord's name can be praised throughout the earth.

But how can we bless others if we are barely eking out enough power to live our own spiritual lives? How can barren lives ever provide help for those who are searching for life and rest? One of the most important questions we face as Christians in the twenty-first century is the question of whether or not we are really living under the full blessing of God.

UNBLOCKING THE BLESSING

According to Scripture, God's blessing can rest on both men and women, because with God there is no gender bias. His blessing can rest on a family, a child, or even unborn offspring. It can prosper a local church in such measure that an entire city or region will feel the effect of God's favor on that congregation. God's blessing can rest on the labor of our hands, our personal finances, or our physical well-being. In fact, Moses told the Israelites that "the LORD your God will *bless you in everything you do*" (Deuteronomy 15:18). Think of the vast potential we have if we live under the blessing of God!

But then again, the blessing of God does *not* automatically rest on every person, family, or church. Some of us live out our years under a closed heaven. Because God doesn't smile on our lives, nothing seems to work as we struggle on year after year. This can be true even for those who have professed faith in Jesus Christ as Savior.

Likewise, Christian churches can live outside God's favor, becoming like the congregation at Laodicea that Christ warned us about: "So, because you are lukewarm—neither hot nor cold—I am about to spit you out of my mouth" (Revelation 3:16). Doesn't exactly sound as if God's blessings were overflowing in that church! Just because "God is love" doesn't mean that all is well with everyone here on planet earth. In fact, it's possible to live life under God's displeasure, even to the point of bringing his curse down upon us. The Word of God speaks clearly about this subject as something that requires sober thought and honest investigation.

Perhaps no one in the history of Israel treasured the blessing of God as much as David, Israel's second and greatest king. Over and again, David proved the maxim that when the Lord's favor is on a man, he triumphs over his enemies no matter how many or how fierce. No wonder David penned this glorious promise: "They may curse, *but you will bless*" (Psalm 109:28). He was saying that God's blessing is invincible against all the powers of earth and hell.

Many of the new believers at Brooklyn Tabernacle have come from countries filled with witchcraft and voodoo. These precious souls will sometimes make an appointment to see me or one of the associate pastors. Some are concerned about a former friend or disgruntled family member who is practicing voodoo against them. A sweet lady once nervously related to me that a witch who lived in her apartment building had placed a dead chicken in front of her door as part of a curse against her! You might be amazed to learn that such things still happen in this day and age, but thank God that we needn't fear them when we are protected by the shield the Lord has put around us. What God blesses, no demon can curse.

How reassuring it is to know that no sorcery can undo the *sure* blessings of our Lord. There is no better illustration of this truth than the story of Balak, king of Moab, and the mysterious prophet named Balaam. King Balak could see that God was with Israel as this numerous people moved toward the Promised Land. Realizing an army could not succeed against them, Balak decided to implement a spiritual strategy by hiring a prophet named Balaam to curse Israel. This proved unsuccessful in the end, but Balaam's inspired prophecy in response to Balak's request merits our careful consideration.

Then Balaam uttered his oracle:

"Balak brought me from Aram,
the king of Moab from the eastern mountains.

'Come,' he said, 'curse Jacob for me;
   come, denounce Israel.'
How can I curse
   those whom God has not cursed?
How can I denounce
   those whom the LORD has not denounced? . . .
"Arise Balak and listen;
   Hear me, son of Zippor.
God is not a man, that he should lie,
   nor a son of man, that he should change his mind.
Does he speak and then not act?
   Does he promise and not fulfill?
I have received a command to bless;
   he has blessed, and I cannot change it. . . .
"There is no sorcery against Jacob,
   no divination against Israel.
It will now be said of Jacob
   and of Israel, 'See what God has done!'"

NUMBERS 23:7–8, 18–20, 23

In truth, nothing can overcome the blessing of God on our lives even though he permits us to face battles along the way. Even the permitted hardships and conflicts we endure against the enemy are part of his plan to bless us. But we need to learn to see them in this more spiritual light. While the Old Testament speaks much about outward, physical blessings from God, the New Testament explores the more important, invisible spiritual blessings that we have in Jesus Christ. These are the blessings that bring us joy and peace, preparing us for eternity with our Lord. But both kinds of blessings are far more important than most of us can imagine.

> Nothing can overcome the blessing of God on our lives even though he permits us to face battles along the way. Even the hardships and conflicts we endure are part of his plan to bless us.

Remember the last part of Balaam's prophecy about the people of God: "It will now be said of Jacob and of Israel, *"See what God has done!"* (Numbers 23:23). The Lord cherishes his people, and out of that love flows his desire to bless them. It is through these unmistakable blessings that others can witness God's goodness and declare, "Look what the Lord has done!" This is the divine strategy for spreading the message of God's greatness and the salvation he offers to mankind. As his blessings overflow into our lives, we become a living display of what only the Lord can accomplish here on earth.

> I would rather live under God's special favor than anything else in the world! The greatest epitaph we can have on our tombstones is simply this: *"He was blessed by God in all he did."*

A Christian filled with peace and joy stands out like a light in a day dominated by fear and depression. Such a person proves that God is greater than the worst kind of terrorist threats or economic uncertainties. A man or woman living under an open heaven is more influential than someone who merely spouts theological arguments with no living reality behind them. Even one local church richly blessed by the Holy Spirit accomplishes more for the kingdom of God than twenty congregations living in spiritual barrenness. Nothing, in fact, can replace the blessing of God upon his people. All the human talent, cleverness, and church-growth methods in the world can never compare with the invisible but very real blessing of God.

The church itself was born nearly two thousand years ago by the blessing of God. Even though the early believers had very few of the advantages we boast of, "the Lord's hand was with them" (Acts 11:21). God's blessing overcame every problem so that the gospel message spread everywhere in power. Because of that, I would rather live under God's special favor than anything else in the world! How else will my preaching make a difference in people's lives? How else can the Brooklyn Tabernacle reach the multitudes living in the emptiness of sin all around it? The greatest epitaph any of us could have on our tombstones is simply this: *"He was blessed by God in all he did."*

THE FIRST SECRET OF BLESSING

What can we do to receive this kind of blessing from God? Is there a secret, and if so, what is it? Fortunately, there are clear biblical directives to guide us. The first obvious instruction from the Lord is that we are *to ask in prayer* for an outpouring of God's favor. You remember what made Jabez stand out in his generation: "Jabez cried out to the God of Israel, 'Oh, that you would bless me ...!'" (1 Chronicles 4:10). Jabez, it seems, could not accept the idea of living *without* the blessing of God. Please notice the emphatic words, "Jabez *cried out.*" His was no mere mental prayer, but the deep cry of a soul that could not live without an open heaven above him.

Jabez's prayer reminds us of Jacob, one of the patriarchs of Israel, who also had a breakthrough time of prayer with God one day. One night Jacob wrestled with God-in-the-form-of-a-man and afterward uttered a sentence that has inspired many people throughout the centuries to fervently seek God for more. As the man sought to leave, Jacob responded, "I will not let you go *unless you bless me*" (Genesis 32:26).

This kind of passionate, desperate prayer is definitely out of vogue today. Maybe that's the reason we experience so little divine blessing on both the church as a whole and her individual members. So often we seem content with the status quo rather than reaching out for more of God. Because of this, we seem to have little effect on the world around us. The sad truth is that most of our churches experience relatively few conversions. Instead, we grieve over large numbers of wayward children, a growing tide of divorce, increased addiction to pornography. All these afflict the church itself—yet even this host of ills can't seem to stir us up enough so that we cry out to God, even wrestling with him if necessary, to secure supernatural help from heaven.

Everywhere I travel, I keep hearing the defensive teaching that fervent, heartfelt prayer is really overrated and not necessary today. Since God is love, some people reason, we just have to ask once and politely for what we need and everything will turn out just fine. No need today for prayer meetings and prolonged times of waiting on the Lord, no sir. No need for anyone to persevere in prayer until the answer comes. No, that's part of an old-fashioned, out-of-date theology that belongs to another era.

Well, I have two questions in response to all that:

1. What do these words from the Bible mean?

> And the Lord said, "Listen to what the unjust judge says. And will not God bring about justice for his chosen ones, *who cry out to him day and night?*" (Luke 18:7).

> During the days of Jesus' life on earth, he offered up prayers and petitions with *loud cries and tears* to the one who could save him from death, and he was heard because of his reverent submission (Hebrews 5:7).

I do not fully understand the mysteries of how a sovereign God answers the petitions of frail human beings, but it does seem clear that effective praying often involves more than just saying the right words. Seeking God with our whole heart is the kind of Bible praying that secures not just answers but the blessing of God that we all need. If Jesus Christ himself prayed with "loud cries and tears" at times, then I can certainly feel free and unashamed in pouring out my own soul to God. And so can you.

2. When it comes to de-emphasizing prayer and the prayer meeting in churches across the land, where are the spiritual results that prove we have found a better way? I understand all the warnings about emotionalism and the importance of sound Bible exposition. But show me any place where the blessing of God is resting on churches in such fullness that large numbers of people are coming under conviction of sin and turning to the Lord in repentance and faith. Isn't that what we all want to see? Isn't that the blessing of God we so sorely need?

We might need to listen to some of the great souls who have gone before us in the faith, who experienced visitations of God's blessing that shook whole communities. One of the illustrious names from that number is David Brainerd, a great missionary to Native Americans in the 1740s before America became a nation. Though faced with severe obstacles (including an interpreter who was often drunk), this young missionary prayed for both personal revival and a great harvest of souls. His journal has inspired countless thousands of people to pray and surrender their lives in service to God.

Monday, April 19 [1742]. I set apart this day for fasting and prayer to God for his grace and for him to prepare me for the work of the ministry. I asked him to give me divine help and direct me in preparing for that great work and to send me into his harvest in his own time.

In the afternoon, God was with me in a special way. Oh, how I enjoyed blessed communion with him! God enabled me so to agonize in prayer until I was quite wet with perspiration although I was in a cool place. My soul was greatly burdened for the world and for the multitudes of souls needing salvation. I think I interceded more for sinners than for the children of God although I felt as if I could spend the rest of my life praying for both. I enjoyed great sweetness in communion with my dear Savior. I think I never felt such an entire separation from this world and more totally surrendered to God. Oh, that I may always trust in and live for my God! Amen.[2]

THE SECOND SECRET OF BLESSING

Another vital channel of blessing comes from God's precious Word, the Bible. I read a certain passage from Revelation many times over before I came to understand its critical significance: "*Blessed* is the one who reads the words of this prophecy, and *blessed* are those who hear it and take to heart what is written in it" (Revelation 1:3). Though this is the introductory passage to the Book of Revelation, I believe this promise of blessing applies to every line of Scripture. A tremendous blessing awaits each of us every day in the Word of God! When we read with a sincere desire to hear God and take his truth to heart by faith, we will receive favor from him.

Think of all the blessings we squander by allowing ourselves to become too busy to spend time with God's Word. Though some believers are in such a woeful backslidden state that they have lost all desire for the Bible, many people want to read it but simply can't find the time. Yet it's more than just a matter of time. Reading the Bible on a regular basis involves engaging in spiritual warfare, because Satan doesn't want us to read it. He knows God intends to bless us through the Bible, so he tries to make us think we are too busy. God help us to defeat him and his crafty strategies to keep us from the blessing that God wants to give us every day as we come into contact with his Word.

Why not ask God today for fresh grace to read the Bible daily? No matter how many times you have failed, request God's help so that a new love relationship will begin between you and the Word of God. Don't let the devil rob you of the blessing the Lord has set before you! Remember, there is real blessing from the Almighty in reading and taking to heart every inspired word of Scripture.

THE THIRD SECRET OF BLESSING

Perhaps the most critical key in opening a channel for the blessing of God is the one we often find the most difficult: the matter of *obedience through faith*. Obedience, of course, is a first principle of spiritual life in Christ: "For surely, O LORD, you *bless the righteous;* you surround them with your favor as with a shield" (Psalm 5:12).

Who are these righteous people who are surrounded and protected by the blessing of God against every weapon and attack of the enemy? They can't be people who are morally perfect, for there are no such people. No, God's blessing is reserved for those who long with all their souls to walk in his light and holiness. The righteous in this context are those who will not tolerate sin in their lives but who are always quick to confess their disobedience and seek mercy from the Lord.

On who else could a holy God pour out his blessings but on those who "hunger and thirst for righteousness" (Matthew 5:6)? Can our heavenly Father shower us with blessings if we cling to and practice the same sins that nailed Jesus Christ to the cross? Will we experience his favor if we continually grieve the Holy Spirit he has given to live within us? Such a thing is an absolute impossibility in the moral universe that God rules over.

That's why King Saul was rejected by the Lord and David put in his place. That's the explanation behind the story of Esau losing his birthright to Jacob and the blessing of God along with it. That's why men and women can enjoy the favor of God for decades, only to lose it—and sometimes their ministries— because sin has become so entrenched in their hearts. To lose this blessing because we prefer to cling to our sins is to suffer the most profound tragedy imaginable.

When God gives his holy commands and issues his personal orders for our lives, it is never because he wants to rain on our parade or spoil our party. Motivated always by love, he wants to keep us under the fountain of his innumerable blessings. He wants to freely give more than we want to receive. But his blessings come with unchangeable conditions and requirements that have their foundation in his holy nature.

God wants us to trust him totally by giving him the reins of our lives. This is why he told his chosen one, Isaac, "Stay in this land for a while, and I will be with you and will *bless* you"

God wants to freely give more than we want to receive. But his blessings come with unchangeable conditions that have their foundation in his holy nature.

(Genesis 26:3). Because Isaac remained where God told him to, the Lord upheld his part of the bargain, smiling down on Isaac's submission and obedience. Even beyond the moral commands of the Bible, God often gives us personal directions so we can stay in the center of his will. How could I make unilateral decisions, without consulting the Lord, and then expect his hand of blessing to follow everywhere *I* want to go?

To obey or disobey? This is the struggle so many of us lose, forfeiting as a result many of the good things the Lord intends. When God clearly reveals a certain path for us to follow, it can become a critical point of obedience upon which hang the blessings of tomorrow. When a remnant of the Jewish people returned to Jerusalem from captivity, the prophets boldly announced that God had made their return possible so that the temple could be rebuilt. Therefore he pronounced a blessing on them the same day they obediently laid the temple foundation: "From *this day* on I will *bless* you" (Haggai 2:19).

The day of obedience became the day of blessing, the moment when God manifested again his bountiful provision for his people. Barrenness was replaced by fruitfulness because the people yielded to God's call on their lives. It's the same today! God is waiting for us to obey by faith the leadings and promptings he so often gives us. As we obey, untold divine resources and grace will be provided. Let us make today the day of blessing, one in which we have a new sense of God's strong hand resting on us.

THE FOURTH SECRET OF BLESSING

There's one more secret to obtaining God's blessing. When Moses was giving his final instructions and farewell address to the Israelites, he gave specific instructions about something called "the third-year tithe." Unlike the regular tithe, or ten percent annual offering, the third-year tithe was reserved for a different purpose.

> At the end of every three years, bring all the tithes of that year's produce and store it in your towns, so that the Levites (who have no allotment or inheritance of their own) and the *aliens, the fatherless and the widows* who live in your towns may come and eat and be satisfied, *and so that the* LORD *your God may bless you* in all the work of your hands (Deuteronomy 14:28–29).

It is important to see what God is doing here. Every third year, the towns of Israel became huge storage centers for the tithes of this agricultural nation. These offerings were not brought to the place where the Lord was worshiped in Jerusalem, but rather were given to supply the needs of the priests from the tribe of Levi, who supervised the official worship. Levites were not allowed to own land and have their own farms, so God insisted that the people provide for them in a special way.

But that was not all. The third-year tithe was also earmarked for the aliens, orphans, and widows who lived in the community. What was so special about these people that they were to receive the same consideration as the priests? For one thing, aliens were often excluded by others, sometimes becoming victims of discrimination. Orphans and widows were also vulnerable and in danger of all kinds of exploitation. Because of these unfortunate facts of life, even among God's people, the third-year tithe was reserved for them.

What a marvelous, compassionate God we have! He always has a special place in his heart for the vulnerable, weak, brokenhearted, and rejected among his people. This provision was especially touching because aliens were not even part of the chosen people of Israel. Yet the Lord looked out for them! Compassion and concern for the downtrodden, then, is not merely part of a "liberal agenda," but is rooted in the very heart of our Creator.

However, there was even more to the third-year tithe than supplying the needs of Levites, aliens, orphans, and widows. Israel was to give generously "so that the LORD your God may *bless* you in all the work of your hands." It seems that the act of joyfully giving to others actually opened up the windows of heaven so that the people themselves could be blessed.

> Can we honestly say God is smiling on our life and labor? If not, why not? After all, the problem is never on the Lord's side.

God still wants to do extraordinary things for followers who imitate him in compassionate giving. How many blessings have we missed out on through stinginess and having a "me-first" attitude? How much more might we receive if compassion and open-handedness characterized our daily living? What a profound and far-reaching truth the Lord revealed to the apostle Paul when he taught that "it is more *blessed* to give than to receive" (Acts 20:35).

Can you and I honestly say God is smiling on our life and labor? If not, why not? After all, the problem is never on the Lord's side. God wants us to seek his blessings diligently, for "he rewards those who earnestly seek him" (Hebrews 11:6). Whenever we experience his fullness, God's name is honored. He wants us to align ourselves with his own holy character by walking "in the light, as he is in the light" (1 John 1:7). He desires to give liberally to us as we learn to have the same attitude toward others.

WHEN GOD IS WITH YOU

Earlier I told the story of a hopeless kid from Puerto Rico whose life seemed cursed until God got a hold of him. My friendship with Nicky Cruz has shown me just how powerful the blessing of God can be.

Several years ago, Nicky and I were working together on an evangelistic crusade in the capital city of Lima, Peru. More than ninety members of our church had come with us to do street work and sing gospel music in the plazas, where crowds would gather to listen. It was a great way to spread the gospel as well as to advertise the evening rallies in the national stadium where Nicky would be speaking.

Everything went well until the day before the crusade. Newspaper, radio, and TV reporters had gathered for a press conference at a ballroom in the Lima Sheraton. I sat next to Nicky at the head table while a translator filled me in on what was being said.

The questions seemed routine enough until one of the reporters stood up and challenged Nicky: "Why do we need a Puerto Rican from the United States to come here and preach to us about the solution to youth violence and drug problems? Who are you, anyway? Isn't the United States the place where most drugs are used, and don't you have enough problems there to work on?"

The room grew suddenly quiet as the man went on in a voice filled with disdain and hostility.

"We in Peru need a former Puerto Rican gang leader to tell us about God? I resent you even being here in our country!"

Next to me, the translator seemed agitated and began praying under her breath. You could feel the tension in the room as all eyes turned toward Nicky, waiting for his response. There were cameras and open microphones everywhere.

"Thank you very much for your honest question," he began. "Let me tell you a little about my life. *I used to like to hurt people*. I got my kicks from messing up people pretty bad. In fact, *I used to like to hurt people just like you.*"

What? Where was Nicky heading? I started praying hard!

"But that was a long time ago, before Jesus changed my life. I didn't come here as an American or as a Puerto Rican, but as a Christian who has been changed by the power of God! You're right, America is a messed up place in many ways, but that's why I leave my wife and four daughters and travel so that people there can hear about the love of Jesus. You live in a beautiful country, but Peru needs Christ just like the rest of the world. And because Jesus changed me from a wild, hate-filled, violent animal on the streets, I want you to know about his power, too."

As Nicky finished, the reporter left his seat and started walking toward the head table. Cameramen drew near to film whatever was about to happen next. *What if the guy threw a punch?* I wondered. *What would Nicky do?*

None of us anticipated what happened next. Stopping squarely in front of Nicky, the reporter extended his hand, a smile on his face.

"Your answer tells me you are an honest man. I will be there tomorrow night to hear you speak." With that, the two men shook hands, and the rest of us sighed our relief.

How an unschooled man like Nicky, raised in the mean streets of Brooklyn, could defuse such a tense situation with perfect poise and wisdom is a testimony to the blessing of God. When the hand of the Lord is with someone, no dilemma is without a divine solution. The same God who has blessed and used Nicky Cruz to help others is able to do the same for you.

NOTES

1. Nicky Cruz, *Run Baby Run* (Plainfield, N.J.: Logos Associates, 1988).
2. Brainerd's journal, first published in London in 1748, is available today in various editions, both complete and abridged.

FOCUS ON THE FAMILY.

GOING
PUBLIC *with*
YOUR FAITH

BECOMING A SPIRITUAL
INFLUENCE AT WORK

WILLIAM CARR PEEL, Th.M.
AND WALT LARIMORE, M.D.

INTRODUCTION

❧

"I want my life to count. I don't want to look back at the end and think I wasted it."

Most of us have heard this sentiment expressed many times. Many of us, the authors included, have expressed it ourselves. The desire to make a positive difference—to be significant—before God is a healthy desire. Those in the church, evangelicals in particular, define this significance largely in terms of their efforts to share the gospel—to spread the Word, to see others at home and abroad come to faith in Jesus Christ.

Unfortunately, few have experienced much success in this area of their Christian lives. Efforts to share Christ seem uncomfortable, awkward, ineffective, perhaps even counterproductive. The formulas and methods for sharing the gospel seem mechanical, unrealistic. They may look good on paper, but they just don't seem to be working. Thus many, despite their desire to carry out this biblical responsibility, have simply given up.

If you have questions about how to share your faith—how to "go public"—this book will help. You will see how the seemingly insignificant words you speak and actions you take can have great significance before God and in the lives of the people you encounter.

WITNESS THE WAYS

As you will soon see, our focus is on our culture's ripest mission field—the workplace. You will encounter others who have gone public in their places of work whose testimonies can instruct and inspire. One such person is George. I (Bill) sat across the table from George as he finished the paperwork for the purchase of my wife's fiftieth-birthday present. He is a jeweler of Lebanese descent whose grandfatherly personality, exotic accent, and love of Jesus make my heart smile every time I visit his store. I asked, "George, what's the favorite part of your job?" He quickly replied, "Helping young couples find a beautiful ring that is just right for them." He explained how, as he does his work, he looks for opportunities to impart some small bit of biblical wisdom about relationships. He pulled out a note from his desk drawer and read a few lines a young bride had recently written:

> Thank you so much for helping us find the beautiful ring and making it possible for us to purchase it. Of all the salespeople who helped us, you seemed to really care about us. And thank you for the advice about marriage. Dick and I have decided we need to find a church to attend. Thanks for your encouragement.

And there is John, a caretaker. Before leaving on a business trip to England, John's boss gave him final instructions: "Take good care of my family, John." The graying caretaker smiled and said, "I will, and I'll pray for your success." The executive paused, looked back, and said, "John, I don't know what I'd do without you. There's no one on this island I trust more than you."

It hadn't always been that way. A great sea of mistrust separates the cultures that John and his employer come from. One was raised in a privileged environment, the son of six generations of plantation owners on the island of Barbados; the other was the son of slaves. When John began working for his wealthy boss ten years ago, he was charged with maintaining the perimeter of the property. He was not allowed to go anywhere near the house. Each year John's hard work and godly character earned him more responsibility. Today John oversees the entire property, entrusted with not only the house and grounds but the well-being of the family when his boss is away on business. John told me he prays daily for this man and his family. "God has allowed me to win my way into his house. Now I pray that God will open their hearts so they may come to know Jesus."

These followers of Jesus in the workplace are passionate about their faith. They love to talk to people about Jesus. But their motive is not to proselytize. Rather it is to discover what God is already doing in someone's life and to join that effort. It is to show Jesus to those with whom they work, not to sell Jesus or force him on others. It is to help others become new creations, not to coerce people to "change religions."

A NEW WAY TO LOOK AT EVANGELISM

Our proposition is simple: For most Christians these days, the workplace—not the church or a foreign mission field—is the primary setting for effective kingdom work. We believe this proposition to be both biblically and historically true. When the church has allowed people to set their focus inside the four walls, it has tended to dwindle in size. But when the church has launched people outward into the world, encouraging them to *go public* with their faith, it has invariably grown. The early church is a prime example. It grew from a handful of disciples in the A.D. 30s to over half a million people by the end of the first century. This growth didn't occur as a result of the proliferation of full-time missionaries; it happened because ordinary followers of Jesus took their faith to the workplace and lived it out in their ordinary everyday encounters. Early Christians chatted about the gospel in bakeries, wine shops, marketplaces, and barracks. From the dusty streets of Jerusalem to the soggy outposts of the British Isles, these early followers of Jesus spread the gospel gladly and with an enthusiasm that could never be produced by wage or sense of duty.

At times God provides other avenues for spreading the gospel. But we contend that the primary historical means God uses to spread the Good News and extend the influence of faith is to "send it to work" with ordinary people. This was our premise in 1995 when we teamed up to write *The Saline Solution,* with the goal of teaching doctors how to talk about their faith with their patients. Ironically, neither of us considered himself a gifted evangelist. Both of us have had thorough training to aggressively present the gospel message to people we didn't know. And even though we had a great desire to share our faith, we broke into a cold sweat when faced with the opportunity to talk about Jesus with non-Christians. What emerged from our collaboration was serious business—a new model of evangelism, a model of spiritual influence that doctors who live under intense time pressure and significant ethical limitations can use every day with every patient. As we taught this approach to doctors, many of whom have a deep passion for spiritual impact, we regularly heard the same three comments: (1) "I feel a load of guilt has been taken off my shoulders," (2) "I can do this!" and (3) "You need to adapt this for other professions besides health care."

This is our goal for this book. We believe the *going public* approach to offering spiritual truth to a lost world is biblical. We believe it will change the way Christians view evangelism and also the way non-Christians view Christians.

As we examined both Scripture and our own experience, we stumbled on a concept that is often ignored by modern evangelistic methods: Evangelism is not an event but a process. That is, evangelism is less about imparting a set of facts about God and humankind and asking a person to make a decision to receive Jesus as Savior on the spot than it is about a process—usually a prolonged process—that begins by preparing or *cultivating* someone's heart to receive that message.

To put it another way, evangelism is organic, not mechanical. Interestingly, the Bible consistently chooses an agrarian model to describe evangelism. Evangelism, after all, is a process comparable to growing a crop: cultivating + planting = harvest. It takes time to cultivate a relationship in which seeds of biblical truth can be planted and can grow, resulting in an eventual harvest of eternal life.

We believe that the bubble has burst for an aggressive, nonrelational approach to evangelism. It's time to go back to the farm for our model. Like growing a crop, evangelism takes diligent work over an extended period of time. There's nothing instant about it. For people who love to "close the deal," such "preliminaries" may seem like a waste of time. But we strongly believe that people today have no more desire to hear from a stranger about how to receive eternal life than they do to invest all their money in the next cold-call stock tip. Skepticism about Christian faith is as prominent today as it has ever been. This is a significant barrier to belief that must be recognized, addressed, and overcome if we expect people to come to faith. To do so takes time.

The journey of faith consists of a multitude of small, incremental decisions regarding spiritual realities. Thus the greatest privilege in the world—being part of someone's journey to Jesus—can begin with something as simple as having a cup of coffee with a colleague, listening compassionately when a customer shares why she's had a rough week, or doing something beyond the call of duty for a boss or employee who's under stress. As you read and interact with the ideas in this book, you will see that small actions and simple attempts to serve others in the course of everyday life have a bigger impact than the "spiritual interruptions" we sometimes seek to orchestrate out of a sense of guilt.

You will also discover that, although you play an important role, it is ultimately *God* who is at work behind the scenes to create opportunities for meaningful discussions about spiritual topics. Our job as God's representatives is not to try to "start a fire in the rain" but to discover where he is already at work and to pour fuel on that fire.

We regularly meet men and women who do not consider themselves evangelists by any stretch of the imagination. Yet they love God deeply and want their lives to count for his kingdom. Our prayer is that you, our readers, will not only recognize the incredible influence you can have right where you are but that you will also experience the unparalleled joy of seeing the people with whom you work come to know Jesus. Oh, and we'd also love to see you set free from guilt and learn to say, with God-given confidence, "I can do this!"

Spiritual Economics

In 1921, President Franklin Delano Roosevelt was stricken with polio, a disease he struggled with until his death in April 1945. On the tenth anniversary of FDR's death, Dr. Jonas Salk announced that the polio vaccine he had developed was ready for use by the general public. Over thirty years later, in the late 1980s, thousands of doses of oral polio vaccine were being stored in drug company refrigerators. Yet hundreds of thousands of polio cases were still being reported around the globe. The supply was plentiful. The problem was a failure of distribution.

In stepped Rotary International, which set a lofty goal—to eradicate polio from the world. The organization raised more than $200 million to buy enough vaccine to meet the entire global need. But they, too, confronted the same massive problem—distribution. Working in conjunction with the World Health Organization, Rotarians developed a strategy that called for identifying the most needy countries and designating "national vaccination days." Thousands of health officials and volunteers vaccinated entire countries against polio in a matter of a day or two. By 2001, only 500 cases of polio were reported worldwide. By addressing the challenge of distribution, the Rotarians have saved thousands from premature death or disability.

Basic economic principles revolve around supply, demand, and distribution. A business enterprise may have abundant capital, solid management, and a worthy product. None of it will matter even a little bit if the enterprise cannot address the challenge of *distribution*. No matter how strong the demand or how abundant the supply in the warehouse, if the enterprise cannot get the product into the hands of the consumer, its demise is inevitable.

Many of the world's problems are a result of failure to meet the challenge of distribution. While the granaries in many developed nations overflow, millions go to bed hungry each night. We've all read the accounts of how rival factions in various Third World countries prevent grain from reaching starving people. The problem is *distribution*—figuring out how to bridge the gap between abundant resources and desperate demand. Tons of much-needed food and water sat in warehouses in Umm Qasr in the spring of 2003 while Iraqis went without basic necessities because Iraq's distribution system was virtually non-existent.

One of the key components to America's prosperity is its distribution system, that is, our ability to identify a need, develop a product or service to meet the need, and then deliver it to the customer quickly and efficiently. Although Sam Walton (the richest man in America until his death in 1992) has been called a retailer, the true key to the success of Wal-Mart is automated distribution. It efficiently delivers goods to its more than 3,200 facilities in the United States and passes on the savings to its more than 100 million weekly customers.[1]

THE SPIRITUAL CHALLENGE

This same dynamic applies to the realm of spiritual resources. All over the world, people are looking as never before for spiritual answers and resources. As human solutions continue to fail, more and more people are seeking divine help. Vaclav Havel, president of the Czech Republic, has said, "Communism has left a vacuum in the hearts of men." Stories of spiritual hunger from the former Soviet bloc pour into the West.

But by no means do the spiritually oppressed in the former Soviet Union have a corner on spiritual need. In 1995 researcher and futurist George Barna estimated that the number of people in the United States who do not have a relationship with Jesus would reach 235 million by 2000,[2] making the U.S. home to the world's fourth largest non-Christian population.

Americans are not so much antispiritual as they are indifferent to religious institutions. In 2000, Barna reported that the number of unchurched adults had been on the rise for three years, leaving one out of three adults unchurched.[3] Nevertheless, there is more openness to spiritual answers today than in previous decades. Two-thirds of unchurched adults want to experience God in a deeper and more tangible and significant way.[4] But Americans are not automatically turning to the church for this experience, as did their grandfathers and grandmothers. Instead they are trying counterfeit spiritual remedies.

THE SUPPLY

If you know the God of the Bible, you certainly know there is no problem on the supply side of the spiritual economics equation. "Now to him who is able to do immeasurably more than all we ask or imagine," wrote the apostle Paul (Ephesians 3:20–21), "according to his power that is at work within us, to him be glory in the church and in Christ Jesus throughout all generations, for ever and ever! Amen."

God's resources are limitless; his grace and love have no boundaries. And he longs to pour out this spiritual wealth on desperate and spiritually needy people. Paul wrote to the Christians in Philippi, "And my God will meet all your needs according to his glorious riches in Christ Jesus" (Philippians 4:19).

Given that we worship a God of *unlimited abundance,* the spiritual problem is clearly *not* a matter of supply. This leaves only one alternative: distribution. Simply put, the ways in which we've been delivering the spiritual goods have not been working. The idea, for example, that we can open a "distribution center" on some street corner and expect those in spiritual need to come to us has not worked. In fact, God did not intend for it to work. God is not in the retail business. He has chosen one-on-one mass distribution as his method to distribute his grace.

GOD'S DISTRIBUTION METHOD

It's fascinating to consider that, of all the methods the Creator of the universe could have used to spread his grace to the world, he chose to use men and women—ordinary Christians—not a few select, elite spokespersons. As he departed this earth, Jesus told his followers, "And you will be my witnesses in Jerusalem, and in all Judea and Samaria, and to the ends of the earth" (Acts 1:8).

God calls you and me as his witnesses, and we do not need to search hard to find a mission field. Our mission field is the place where we already spend most of our time, namely, our workplace. By being an ambassador for Jesus in the workplace, each of us can become a pipeline of God's grace to people who would never darken the doorway of a church. Now *that* is distribution!

God wants to use us to accomplish something so grand we can hardly imagine its significance. For each person this *something to be accomplished* is totally unique. Sound daunting? Relax! God has given you everything you need.

Evangelism as a Process

Many Christians of our generation were taught mechanical, aggressive (some would say intrusive) methods of evangelism that produced minimal results, despite the claims made by the organizations espousing these methods. I (Bill), motivated partly by guilt, took part in several evangelism seminars or courses, but the results became predictable.

> The longer I am in business, the more passionate I become to be the hands, the feet extended of Christ. I see so many people who have not known God, don't think about God, don't talk about God. I want to provoke people to at least think about God. I want them to experience the love of Christ through me.
>
> ANNE BEILER

I would get inspired, go out and try what I'd learned, fail, stop trying—and feel even more guilty. I finally concluded that I just wasn't gifted to share my faith with others, which made me feel like a substandard Christian.

In the medical arena, I (Walt) found that an aggressive approach to evangelism was not only uncomfortable (both for me and my patients) but was also largely unfruitful. One day I just quit trying, content to consider my practice as merely a secular "tentmaking" operation while carrying on my ministry in the context of church life. Yet my heart was troubled. Every day I saw twenty to thirty non-Christian patients who desperately needed both physical and spiritual healing, and I came to believe I had nothing to offer them in the latter area.

The problem was that, as with many Christians, we (both authors) thought of evangelism as an *event*—a point in time when we mechanically recite the facts of the gospel message and encourage non-Christians to place their faith in Jesus. It was liberating for each of us to discover that evangelism, according to the Bible, is not an event but a *process*. Evangelism is organic—a lot more like farming than selling. This concept radically changed our lives and our ministries—Walt's in medicine and Bill's in professional ministry.

Event-centered evangelism defines success as getting a person to pray to receive Jesus as personal Savior. But when evangelism is seen as an organic process, this "decision" is only the climactic step of a long process that God uses to draw a person to himself. God's process typically enlists a number of people with a variety of gifts—each playing a different but vital role in helping someone take a step closer to Jesus. Accepting God's gift of salvation—obviously the goal of evangelism—is dependent on many steps before it. Bill Kraftson of Search Ministries observes that each Christian who encounters a non-Christian is like a link in a chain. "It's great to be the last link in the chain," says Kraftson, "but it's not more important than any other link. We just need to make sure we're not the missing link." Jim Petersen of the Navigators likewise views conversion as a process: "Few of us make it in one big decision. Instead, it is a multitude of small choices—mini-decisions that a person makes toward Jesus."[5]

THE DISTRIBUTION PROCESS

The Bible consistently employs an organic rather than a mechanical model to explain how God draws a person to himself. Paul uses the agrarian analogy in his passionate comments about the growing factions competing in the Corinthian church:

> What, after all, is Apollos? And what is Paul? Only servants, through whom you came to believe—as the Lord has assigned to each his task. I planted the seed, Apollos watered it, but God made it grow. So neither he who plants nor he who waters is anything, but only God, who makes things grow. The man who plants and the man who waters have one purpose, and each will be rewarded according to his own labor. For we are God's fellow workers; you are God's field, God's building.
>
> 1 Corinthians 3:5–9

MICRODECISIONS OF FAITH[6]

DISCIPLE	Chooses to live by faith	**+ 5**	**MULTIPLYING**	SPEAKS TO: THE WHOLE PERSON ADDRESSES: SOCIAL BARRIERS TO OVERCOME: ISOLATION BY: PARTICIPATION IN THE BODY GOAL: GROWTH ANSWERS: WILL I LIVE FOR CHRIST? EXAMPLES: JERUSALEM CHURCH (ACTS 2:41-47) THE CHURCH AT ANTIOCH (ACTS 11:19-26)
	Chooses to share faith	**+ 4**		
	Makes Christlike choices	**+ 3**		
BELIEVER	Joins in community life	**+ 2**		
	Assimilates God's Word	**+ 1**		
SEEKER	Trusts in Christ	**0**	**HARVESTING**	SPEAKS TO: THE WILL ADDRESSES: VOLITIONAL BARRIERS TO OVERCOME: INDECISION & UNWILLINGNESS TO CHANGE BY: PRAYER & PERSUASION GOAL: TRUST CHRIST ANSWERS: WILL I TRUST CHRIST? EXAMPLES: PAUL BEFORE AGRIPPA (ACTS 26:1-29)
	Turns from self-trust	**- 1**		
	Sees Christ as the answer	**- 2**		
	Recognizes spiritual need	**- 3**		
SPECTATOR	Considers the truth of the gospel	**- 4**	**PLANTING**	SPEAKS TO: THE MIND ADDRESSES: INTELLECTUAL BARRIERS TO OVERCOME: IGNORANCE, MISCONCEPTIONS & ERROR BY: PRESENTATION GOAL: UNDERSTANDING ANSWERS: WHO IS JESUS? WHAT DOES HE WANT FROM ME? EXAMPLES: ETHIOPIAN EUNUCH (ACTS 8:26-39)
	Understands the implications	**- 5**		
	Aware of the gospel	**- 6**		
	Recognizes relevance of the Bible	**- 7**		
SKEPTIC	Looks positively at the Bible	**- 8**	**CULTIVATING**	SPEAKS TO: THE EMOTIONS ADDRESSES: EMOTIONAL BARRIERS TO OVERCOME: DENIAL, INDIFFERENCE, FEAR & ANTAGONISM BY: YOUR PRESENCE GOAL: ATTRACTION, TRUST YOU ANSWERS: WHAT'S IN IT FOR ME? EXAMPLES: WOMAN AT THE WELL (JOHN 4:4-30) NICODEMUS (JOHN 3:1-21) MATTHEW 13:1-23
	Recognizes difference in the messenger	**- 9**		
	Aware of the messenger	**- 10**		
CYNIC	Going his/her own way	**- 11**		
	Avoids the truth	**- 12**		

After speaking with the Samaritan woman at the well, Jesus uses the organic model to teach his disciples about the process of evangelism. The disciples were about to lead people to Jesus—or as he puts it, "reap" in a field that had previously been cultivated and planted by others:

> Do you not say, "Four months more and then the harvest"? I tell you, open your eyes and look at the fields! They are ripe for harvest. Even now the reaper draws his wages, even now he harvests the crop for eternal life, so that the sower and the reaper may be glad together. Thus the saying "One sows and another reaps" is true. I sent you to reap what you have not worked for. Others have done the hard work, and you have reaped the benefits of their labor.
>
> John 4:35–38

Jesus also uses an agrarian analogy to explain why some people respond to the word of God while others don't:

> A farmer went out to sow his seed. As he was scattering the seed, some fell along the path, and the birds came and ate it up. Some fell on rocky places, where it did not have much soil. It sprang up quickly, because the soil was shallow. But when the sun came up, the plants were scorched, and they withered because they had no root. Other seed fell among thorns, which grew up and choked the plants. Still other seed fell on good soil, where it produced a crop—a hundred, sixty or thirty times what was sown.
>
> Matthew 13:3–8

The seed—"the message about the kingdom" (Matthew 13:19)—falls on soils at varying stages of cultivation, representing the varying degrees of readiness of the human heart. The path—representing hard, uncultivated hearts—can't receive God's word. The rocky places and thorny soils—partially cultivated hearts—receive the words, but life can't flourish. The good soil—well-cultivated hearts—brings forth an abundant harvest.

Jesus' point is clear: A person's journey toward a relationship with him and the experience of eternal life is a process—a long process.

And as with raising a crop, a lot of hard work is required before there is any talk of harvesting.

JESUS' GUIDE TO ORGANIC EVANGELISM

Based on an agrarian model, evangelism can be divided into four phases: cultivating, planting, harvesting, and multiplying. According to Jesus, the hard work of evangelism is not the harvest phase but the *cultivation* phase. Cultivation focuses on the soil of the human heart, which includes addressing emotional barriers. It requires our presence with non-Christians. The goal of cultivation is to help others begin to see the benefits of being a child of God. An important part of cultivation is to develop trust in the messenger, for if people don't trust us, they will never trust our message. Thus, the first step entails building relationships and then living in a way that creates trust. This does not mean we must live impeccable lives, which is something that can't be done anyway. But we can live authentically and honestly—demonstrating to others that we ourselves are in need of grace.

The *planting* phase addresses intellectual barriers—misconceptions, misinformation, and ignorance about God and the Christian faith. It requires thoughtful conversation as part of planting seeds of biblical truth, seeds designed to build an understanding of who Jesus is, what he wants from us, and what he wants to do for us. As we develop relationships with non-Christians and they become attracted to what Jesus is doing in us, we can begin to explain how Jesus has made, and continues to make, a difference in our lives. It begins slowly, with just enough truth to pique interest. As curiosity grows, so does the appetite for the truth. As non-Christians come to grips with spiritual truth, they are likely to discover significant discrepancies between the Bible and their way of thinking or philosophy of life. They'll need answers—presented patiently and humbly—to their intellectual questions.

The *harvesting* phase focuses on a person's will and its resistance to make a decision to trust Jesus. Even after someone's emotional and intellectual barriers have been broken down, the will remains. Men and women can neither think nor feel their way into God's kingdom. Though these elements are foundational, ultimately every human being must make a choice. Involvement during this phase requires prayer and continued conversation toward the goal of the person's receiving Jesus as Savior. In harvesting, we graciously persuade and consistently pray for God to draw our friend to himself.

The final phase, *multiplying*, entails implanting the new life into a community where it can grow and flourish. The goals of this phase are growth and reproduction. When new life is birthed, we need to give it proper care, ensuring that it has an environment that encourages growth and development toward maturity.

WHAT'S RIGHT FOR YOUR WORKPLACE?

If our efforts to go public are to bear fruit, they must take into account contemporary cultural attitudes as well as realities in the twenty-first-century workplace. People are under pressure; schedules are tight. Each working environment is distinctive; relationships between and among supervisors and subordinates, or between employees and clients or patients, vary. A cookie-cutter approach to evangelism is doomed. In fact, some of the old gospel-sharing methods are unwise, if not flat-out unethical. A workable model for evangelism must respect the nonbeliever's integrity and vulnerability while also considering the professional's fiduciary responsibility.

> As a younger Christian, I was much more aggressive about sharing my faith. Now I am much more aware that it is God's work. I am just trying to be faithful on a day-to-day basis. I am much more cautious, because the battle is severe, and if it ever becomes known organizationally that you have an agenda, you can get in trouble.
>
> JACK ALEXANDER, TRAVEL AND HOSPITALITY INDUSTRY

We have found that when people who are not gifted evangelists overemphasize the harvesting phase, they produce more frustration than fruit. They may even further harden the soil of unbelieving hearts. However, when these same men and women exercise their God-given gifts in the cultivating phase of evangelism, they have many more planting and harvesting opportunities. Evangelism is organic. Although this may come as a surprise to some, it is no surprise to any farmer—or to God.

All of us who follow Jesus must think carefully about how we can best make him known in our own workplace, given its particular limitations and constraints. Some work environments afford greater freedom and flexibility to spend time talking about spiritual topics. Others (such as a doctor's office) are highly scheduled and restrictive, allowing virtually no time for prolonged conversations. Some work environments are even hostile with regard to spiritual talk. Those who have a fiduciary responsibility and hold a professional knowledge unavailable to those they serve must take great care not to exploit another's position or situation. Whatever your arena, and however aggressive your workplace may allow you to be, being a "religious jerk" is never appropriate!

Throughout history and today we have witnessed various models for evangelism. We have identified five.

The *proclamational evangelism* model features public preaching and announcing the truth to a large audience. The best-known proclamational evangelist of our time is Billy Graham. Proclamation is modeled in the New Testament by John the Baptist, Jesus, Peter, Stephen, and Paul—all of whom preached the gospel to audiences.

Confrontational evangelism occurs when someone initiates a conversation with an individual (usually a stranger) with the specific aim of leading the person to Jesus. The Bible includes a few examples of this kind of evangelism: Jesus with Nicodemus, Jesus with the Samaritan woman, and Philip with the Ethiopian eunuch. Campus Crusade for Christ popularized this model. In the 1960s and 1970s, when the great search for truth was on at the university campus, this method fit the culture perfectly and was instrumental in both Bill's and Walt's journey of faith and understanding of the gospel.

Though many people are intimidated by talking to people they've never met, there are Christians who love to talk to perfect strangers about Jesus. They come back from business trips with incredible stories about how they met this or that stranger and led him or her in a dramatic way to Jesus. It's easy to think of these individuals as the gifted evangelists who are set apart to carry out the bulk of evangelistic activity for God.

While some people may be ready to hear about Jesus, not as many people are as ready to hear about Jesus from a perfect stranger as they once were. While making the gospel clear, the danger of confrontation is twofold. First, if a person feels pressure to respond before he or she is ready, the experience can create another emotional barrier that must be overcome before the person will trust Jesus. Second, when people who are not gifted evangelists force themselves into this mold, the result is rarely a positive experience—for the evangelist or the evangelized.

Intentional evangelism refers to creating opportunities to expose friends and colleagues to Jesus in a nonreligious, nonthreatening atmosphere. It's what Matthew (also known as Levi) did when he became a follower of Jesus. Instead of inviting his disreputable friends to the synagogue, he asked them to his home for dinner (see Luke 5:27–29).

In the intentional evangelism model, someone hosts a nonthreatening event that creates in non-Christian friends a sense of curiosity, which the host can intentionally pursue after the event. The event is more about sparking an interest than making converts. Intentional evangelism is based on forming a relationship of significant trust with a non-Christian friend and on the hope that the event will stimulate the non-Christian without causing him or her to feel "set up." This usually means that the event will not feature a pushy appeal to trust Jesus.

Events might feature a speaker that non-Christians would be interested in hearing. For several years I (Bill) hosted what we called the Leadership Breakfast during the pro-am golf tournament in Tyler, Texas. Several of the touring pros from the PGA are believers. Each year we invited one of them to talk a little about golf and to tell his faith story. Christians were encouraged to host a table and invite friends. More than three hundred men and women, many of whom wouldn't dream of attending church, came to hear a professional golfer. Another type of intentional evangelistic event is a forum, or discussion party. Rather than focusing on a speaker, this gathering is centered around discussion of questions people have about God or Christianity. Search Ministries and the Alpha course are two examples.

Passive evangelism uses symbols, objects, or art to arouse curiosity in the observer. We sometimes call this "trotline evangelism," after the fishing practice of baiting a series of hooks on a line, then leaving and coming back later to check the line. You put out the bait and hope a fish—or, in the case of evangelism, a person—bites. Religious art on the wall, tracts and magazines left in offices and waiting rooms, even Bibles, are conspicuously placed in hopes that someone may ask a question about God. The Old Testament is full of symbols designed to create curiosity, and many aspects of the Jewish ceremonial law were designed to draw people toward asking questions. Even the temple in Jerusalem was, in some sense, a giant symbolic tract designed to teach people how to approach God.

The benefit of this model is that it's always at work, even when you're not. It continues to say something even while you are absent or silent. The drawback is that it lacks subtlety. What's more, if the office atmosphere doesn't match the decor, a credibility problem arises. If you announce by what you put on the walls that you are a follower of Jesus, you'd better be sure to reflect the values of Jesus in the way you speak and act.

Relational evangelism builds a bridge of friendship based on common ground between a Christian and non-Christian. Relational evangelists see evangelism as a process rather than an event. In this model, success is measured on the basis of helping a person take one more step toward Jesus today.

This type of evangelism was the backbone of the strategy that resulted in the growth of the early church from a few hundred on the day of Pentecost to over half a million by the end of the first century. Christians everywhere chatted about Jesus to their friends, relatives, work associates, customers, masters, slaves, and fellow soldiers. According to church growth experts Win and Charles Arn, "Webs of *common kinship* (the larger family), *common friendship* (friends and neighbors), and *common associates* (work associates and people with common interests or recreational pursuits) are still the paths most people follow in becoming Christians today."[7]

The Arns cite the results of a survey in which approximately 14,000 people were asked the question, "What or who was responsible for your coming to Christ and your church?"[8] Eight responses were rated as follows:

1. A "special need" drew them   1–2 percent
2. They just "walked in"   2–3 percent
3. A pastor   5–6 percent

4. Church "visitation"	1–2 percent
5. Sunday school	4–5 percent
6. Evangelistic crusade or television show	0.5 percent
7. A church "program"	2–3 percent
8. A "friend/relative"	75–90 percent

The results of this survey highlight the importance of forming solid relationships (friendships) as part of the process of evangelism, regardless of which of the above models of evangelism you may employ.

This book explores the specifics of how to engage actively and fruitfully in the evangelistic task. The *fact* that we ought to be engaged in this task should not be an issue. After all, another person's eternal destiny is at stake: Revelation 20:15 declares, "If anyone's name was not found written in the book of life, he was thrown into the lake of fire."

The decision to go public affects believers as well. To refuse to join God as a distribution point of his grace is an act of blatant disregard for God's will and plan for our lives. We cannot stop the flow of grace without doing harm to ourselves. Paul singles out the sharing of our faith as a key to our mature spiritual identity: "I pray that you may be active in sharing your faith, so that you will have a full understanding of every good thing we have in Christ" (Philemon 6).

Certain functions are essential for human life—breathing, drinking, and eating being among them. These functions keep us alive and growing. If we want to remain spiritually alive and growing, we *must* speak of our faith with others. It's a sustaining requirement of spiritual life.

We are all workers in the Father's field. When we go public with our faith in our workplace, we join in his process of drawing men and women to himself. For most of us, it won't involve preaching to groups or aggressively talking to strangers about their relationship with Jesus. Instead, it will focus on the *cultivating* phase, doing what Jesus called "the hard work" (John 4:38)—building meaningful relationships with people over time.

THE BOTTOM LINE												

Evangelism is not an event but a relational process, and God has gifted each of us to play a critical role in drawing men and women to himself.

NOTES

1. "News: Wal-Mart Stores at a Glance" (available at http://www.walmart stores.com/wmstore/wmstores/Mainnews).

2. George Barna, *Evangelism That Works* (Ventura, Calif.: Regal, 1995), 127.

3. "Unchurched People" (available at http://www.barna.org/cgi-bin/PageCategory.asp?CategoryID=38).

4. Barna, *Evangelism That Works*, 58.

5. Cited in K. C. Hinckley, *Living Proof: A Small Group Video Series Discussion Guide* (Chattanooga, Tenn.: Christian Business Men's Committee and NavPress, 1990), 29.

6. This chart was adapted from *Living Proof Video Participant's Guide* (two-part video series published by CMBC, International) and James F. Engel, *What's Gone Wrong with the Harvest?* (Grand Rapids: Zondervan, 1975).

7. Win and Charles Arn, *The Master's Plan for Making Disciples* (Grand Rapids: Baker, 1998), 45–46.

8. Arn and Arn, *The Master's Plan for Making Disciples*, 46.

Every *Child* *Needs a*
Praying Mom

Fern Nichols With Janet
Kobobel Grant

Founder and President of **MOMS IN TOUCH INTERNATIONAL**

Like me, you may have found that one of the most difficult circumstances to pray in is the situation that seems impossible, such as a long-term illness, a rebellious teen, or a spiritually estranged spouse. To keep praying—no matter what—requires a faithfulness of us that's hard to come up with day after day. In the following chapter, I talk about prevailing prayer—how to keep praying while in the storms of life, when you are weary and want to give up. Let this chapter encourage you and give you hope to hold onto a God who cares and loves you passionately.

I've included some suggested prayer for varying situations because part of the challenge is to think of *what* to pray when you feel as though you've uttered your heart's desire in every way possible. And I discuss a situation that kept me on my knees for longer than I imagined I could be and the ways my confidence in prayer were shaken—and how they were resolved. May this chapter help you to resolve to keep praying—no matter what.

Fern Nichols

12. Keep Praying No Matter What!

Lynne wondered if she would ever see a change in her daughter's unhappy life. She says, "Julie was one of those rebellious teenagers who couldn't be told anything but had to experience all the bad things for herself. My prayer group prevailed in prayer for her through the years of her depression, self-mutilation, and suicide attempts. My prayer partners didn't even give up when three days after her eighteenth birthday she married a man, who one week later began an affair and then physically abused her.

"Ten months after she married, she divorced her husband and went back to the college she had dropped out of to marry him. That was a huge answer to prayer because it took a lot of courage to return to a setting where all the kids knew what had happened.

"Then Julie was invited on a weekend camping trip with about fifteen other students. But she decided not to go when she found out they were planning to get drunk and high. My prayer group then asked God to stop the students from going on the trip.

"Julie called me the day of the trip. 'Mom, it's raining so hard I can't even see across the parking lot to the next dorm.' I said, 'Did the other kids go camping?' 'Of course not. It's been pouring all day.' I then told her our group had prayed the Lord would keep them from making the trip. She was quiet for a minute and then asked, 'Do you mean you all can pray and make it rain?' Needless to say, I got quite a laugh out of that.

"After years of running from the Lord, Julie finally surrendered her life to God. Julie dropped by the house as our prayer group was started to pray. I told her I was sorry I couldn't talk to her right then. She said, 'Mother, did you tell those moms they saved my life?' 'Yes, Julie, I did.'"

God says, "Those who hope in me will not be disappointed" (Isaiah 49:23). What a wonderful promise for moms who carry heavy burdens for their children. We are even told by Paul in Romans 12:12 to be "joyful in hope," for "faith is being sure of what we hope for and certain of what we do not see" (Hebrews 11:1).

Prevailing Prayer

During life's storms, when our children aren't walking with the Lord, or when a debilitating illness persists, or when a husband loses his job, we cling to God's words by faith. His words are our lifeline, and prayer is our lifeboat.

What is prevailing prayer? Prevailing prayer is persistent prayer. It's devoting ourselves to stay the course until the answer comes (Colossians 4:2). It's believing that our prayers will transform other's lives. It's *tiptoe anticipation, just waiting for the God of heaven and earth to burst forth with the answer.*

> *Prevailing prayer is tiptoe anticipation, just waiting for the God of heaven and earth to burst forth with the answer.*

And prevailing prayer is the wrestling kind of prayer that Jacob engaged in with the angel in Genesis 32:24. He wrestled, he wept, and he prayed (Hosea 12:4). His faith wasn't shaken, even though the blessing was detained. He wrestled not in his own strength, nor did he prevail in his own strength but God's strength.

Consider the following encouragements to prevail in prayer.

> "Will he plead against me with great power? No, but he would put strength in me" (Job 23: 6, KJV).
>
> It's "not by might nor by power, but by my Spirit, says the LORD Almighty" (Zechariah 4:6).
>
> "In the same way, the Spirit helps us in our weakness. We do not know what we ought to pray for, but the Spirit himself

intercedes for us with groans that words cannot express"
(Romans 8:26).

That's how we pray for our children! Hold on fervently, earnestly,
passionately, intensely, vehemently. Like Jacob, we can decide to not
let go until God blesses our child—until He answers. By God's strength
we will prevail. "Lord, I will not leave You unless You bless my children." Prayer like that is born out of passion for God; He is our only
hope. What heart issues do you need to prevail in prayer about?

Prevailing prayer is hanging onto God's promises until the answer
comes, no matter how long it takes. As Gary Bergel, president of
Intercessors for America, says, we pray "until He settles, resolves, fin-
ishes or initiates a Kingdom solution to an appointed matter."[1] A prevailing intercessor trusts God's timing for the answer. She knows that
with God a thousand years are like a day (Psalm 90:4).

One mom decided her child's school needed a group to pray for it,
but despite placing information about forming a group in the newspaper and making announcements at church, no other mom came to
join her. Each week, this mom faithfully set up chairs in the meeting
room and then proceeded to pray by herself for an hour. And each
week her daughter would ask her, "Did anyone come to pray with
you?" The mom answered, "Jesus sat in one of those chairs." After
four years of being a one-mom group, she finally was joined by
twelve other women.

Let's take seriously Jesus' command: "They ought always to pray
and not to turn coward—faint, lose heart and give up" (Luke 18:1,
AMP). Persevering prayer brings us closer to God. We need the comfort of His voice, the reassurance of His presence. That's what my husband's favorite verse says to us. "But those who hope in the LORD will
renew their strength. They will soar on wings like eagles; they will run
and not grow weary, they will walk and not be faint" (Isaiah 40:31).

God's Part, Our Part

As I read Jean Fleming's book, *A Mother's Heart*, in which she
recounted a story in 2 Kings, I realized how suited that story was to

praying. It reminded me that, while we can do some things, other things only God can do.

Three kings joined forces to fight against the Moabites. As these armies were chasing the enemy, they found themselves in the middle of the desert without water. They and their animals were dying of thirst. Elisha the prophet was sent to inquire of the Lord what to do.

Elisha said, "This is what the LORD says: Make this valley full of ditches. For this is what the LORD says: You will see neither wind nor rain, yet this valley will be filled with water, and you, your cattle and your other animals will drink. This is an easy thing in the eyes of the LORD" (2 Kings 3:15–18).

If the people wanted water, they had to dig the ditches. Their tongues were sticking to the roofs of their mouths, their lips were parched, and their brows were sweaty. All of them were weary, some probably fainted as they worked. But to witness the miracle, they had to do their part.

> *We must settle in our hearts that, no matter what, our Lord tells us to keep praying—right up to the end.*

How long and how deep were those ditches? We don't know. What we do know is "the next morning, about the time for offering the sacrifice, there it was—water flowing from the direction of Edom; and the land was filled with water" (v. 20).

We must settle in our hearts that, no matter what, our Lord tells us to keep praying—right up to the end. First Peter 4:7 says, "The end of the world is coming soon. Therefore, be earnest and disciplined in your prayers" (NLT). When God comes back to Earth, He wants to find His bride praying.

Sometimes do you feel hopeless, that your faith is weak, and that your strength is depleted? Jesus says, even then, keep talking to Him. Yes, even if you have lost heart. For no one understands like Jesus. "We do not have a high priest who is unable to sympathize with our weaknesses, but we have one who has been tempted in every way, just as we are—yet was without sin. Let us then approach the throne of grace with confidence, so that we may receive mercy and find grace to help us in our time of need" (Hebrews 4:15–16).

You could have the privilege of going to Jesus on behalf of a dear friend who is suffering from a long-term illness such as multiple sclerosis. While you could pray for her healing, you might also pray that God will give her the grace to endure her cross, that her inner being would be strengthened with Holy Spirit power, that she would see her Savior in ways she has never seen Him before, that she understands and knows how wide, long, and deep Jesus' love is for her. But most importantly, whatever you pray for her, prevail in your prayers, don't stop.

You can also prevail in prayer for people whose lives brush against yours for a brief time. For example, I'm praying for a young woman my daughter-in-love met in the doctor's waiting room. This girl was all alone, eight months pregnant, and with cancer in her uterus. The doctors want her to abort her baby. I pray for her salvation and that God would bring people into her life to love her and to help. That the Prince of Peace would be at home in her heart.

So many situations require prevailing prayer. These people need others who will cry out day and night to God. As Isaiah 62:6 says, "I have posted watchmen on your walls, O Jerusalem; they will never be silent day or night. You who call on the LORD, give yourselves no rest."

A God Eager to Help

Not praying because we aren't sure what to pray isn't the right choice. We must trust the Holy Spirit to interpret our fumbling thoughts perfectly before the Father. If we only understood how much God wants to help.

Spurgeon writes what he envisions as God's response when we pray.

It is but a small thing for Me, your God, to help you. Consider what I have done already. What! Not help you? Why, I bought you with My blood. What! Not help you? I have died for you; and if I have done that greater, will I not do the less? Help you! It is the least thing I will ever do for you; I have done more, and will do more. Before the world began, I chose you. I made the covenant for you; I laid aside My glory and became a man for you; I gave My life for you; and if I did all this, I will surely help you now. In helping you, I am giving you what I have bought for you already. If you had need of a thousand times as much help, I would give it to you; you require little compared with what I am ready to give. 'Tis much for you to need, but it is nothing for me to bestow.[2]

How can we not trust a God like that?

Recently I was driving through a long stretch of road with grain fields on both sides. I happened to see one lone tree way off in the distance. It was leaning at a forty-five degree angle. Day after day, year after year, the tree slowly had succumbed to the prevailing winds that blew across the plain.

Our prevailing prayers are like the wind of the Holy Spirit, causing the object of our prayer to bend before its persistent force. On any given day we may not see the effects of our prayers; nonetheless, God is at work.

Let's Pray

Praying for long-term, not-easily-resolved issues tries our patience, our faith, and our creativity. After awhile it's hard to know *what* to pray. Using Scripture for your prayers helps you to persevere. In the following scriptural prayers you can insert the person's name into the blanks. Know that God promises you that His word will not return empty. No matter how long it takes for the answer to come, Jesus encourages you to "always pray and not give up" (Luke 18:1).

For prodigals

Gracious Father, reach down your hand from on high and deliver _____ and rescue him from the mighty waters, from

---

the hands of foreigners whose mouths are full of lies, whose right hands are deceitful. (Psalm 144:7–8)

For husbands

My faithful Father, I pray that you will give _____ an undivided heart and put a new spirit in him; please remove from _____ a heart of stone and give him a heart of flesh. Then _____ will follow Your decrees and will be careful to keep Your laws. May _____ know that You are his God. (Ezekiel 11:19–20)

For long-term illness

Dear merciful Lord, I ask that you would strengthen _____ according to Your glorious might so that _____ may have great endurance and patience. (Colossians 1:11)

For salvation

Loving Father, I ask that you would open _____'s eyes and turn him from darkness to light, and from the power of Satan to God, so that he might receive forgiveness of sins and a place among those who are sanctified by faith. (Acts 26:18)

For anxieties

Heavenly Father, I pray in Jesus' name that _____ would not be anxious or fret about anything, but that in everything, he would through prayer and petition with thanksgiving, present his requests to You. Thank You for the promise, that You will grant to _____ Your peace that transcends all understanding, and that You will guard his heart and mind in Christ Jesus. (Philippians 4:6–7)

A Time for Action, a Time for Prayer

But sometimes we have trouble waiting for the answer. Instead of trusting, we step in and take matters in our own hands. When we do, we run the risk of stepping in where God may have intended something altogether different. Before we act, we need to ask God what He wants us to do—or to refrain from doing.

We're like the little boy who found a cocoon. He sat for a while and watched the butterfly struggle to force its body through a small hole. The boy thought it was sad that the butterfly had to work so hard with seemingly little results. So he decided to help. Taking a pair of scissors, he snipped the strands of the cocoon that still held the butterfly imprisoned. The cocoon fell open and out crawled the butterfly. But its body was swollen and had small, shriveled wings. It never could fly. What the boy didn't understand was that the intense struggle to break free was needed to initiate circulation in its wings.

Many of our children struggle to find their own faith. Our job is to love them unconditionally and prevail in prayer. As we seek God, we must ask Him to give us the wisdom to know when to step in and when to keep silent. I know this isn't easy. But rest assured that your loving God is right there with you, scooping up your hurting puddle of a heart and carrying you close to His heart. As Scripture says, "And the one the LORD loves rests between his shoulders" (Deuteronomy 33:12).

Oh, moms, isn't that wonderful? If we do our work—the work of prayer—if we persevere, digging the ditch, one great day water will appear—the answer to prayer. The miracle isn't hard for God.

On his radio program, Ron Hutchcraft gives hurting parents hope as he reminds them of the story found in Luke 7.

> As Jesus approached the gate of a town called Nain, "a dead person was being carried out—the only son of his mother, and she was a widow. And a large crowd from the town was with her. When the Lord saw her, His heart went to her and He said, 'Don't cry.' Then he went up and touched the coffin and those carrying it stood still. He said, 'Young man, I say to you, get up!' The dead man sat up and began to talk, and Jesus gave him back to his mother."
>
> If Jesus can raise a child from the dead to return him to his mother, don't you think He can bring your son or daughter

back from wherever they have wandered? Jesus is calling out to you this very day to say, "Don't give up. Don't lose hope. I've heard your prayers. I'm after him. I'm after her."[3]

Hope is restored when others pray with you. Something wonderful happens when many are praying and tenaciously holding on to the one being prayed for.

The Cumulative Effect

"Our prayers have an accumulative effect," says author Wesley Duewel. "When a dam is erected in a mountain valley, its construction may take many months. Then the water begins accumulating behind the dam, which can take months or even a year or longer. But when the water level reaches the right height, the sluice gates are opened, water begins to turn the generators, and there is tremendous power."

Duewel likens this illustration to persistent, one-accord prayer. "As more and more people unite in prayer or as the prevailing person prays on and on, it seems as if a great mass of prayer is accumulated until suddenly there is a breakthrough and God's will is accomplished. . . . Prayers prayed in the will of God are never lost but are stored until God gives the answer."[4]

The person standing on the dry side of the dam can't see the water accumulating. Then, when that last drop brings the water to the right level, all power breaks lose. Often we stand on the dry side, praying faithfully for a breakthrough in a child's life or our husband's job or our church's disunity or our school being a lighthouse for Jesus. And seemingly nothing happens. But God has heard every prayer, and at His appointed time, all of His power breaks lose.

"I remember literally shaking my fist at God," Jan says as she recounts her prayers for her son, Luke. "He sent me the wrong kid. I wasn't supposed to have a teenager like this—angry, defiant, sneaky, worldly. I had plans to be the world's best mom; how could I have this impossible son?

"As a child, Luke was a joyous, exuberant son but challenging, always pushing. I took comfort in his strong will, thinking he would be strong in resisting peer pressure. Little did I know that most children who are labeled 'strong-willed' actually are *self*-willed, and a self-centered, self-conscious adolescent doesn't want to be different. That was Luke. Living for self and independence, ignoring curfews and courtesies, taking up cigarettes and marijuana, pushing the patience of teachers and parents to the limit.

"I have prayed for Luke all his life, but I'm so grateful that when he was in the third grade, God brought in reinforcements—Moms In Touch. From age eight, those other moms agreed with me before the Father on behalf of my son, had faith when mine was weak, loved him through prayer.

"In our prayer group we pray a bold prayer: that our children will be caught when guilty. I thought many of our prayers fell on God's deaf ears, but *that* prayer God answered over and over again. Luke often was caught in his illegal actions.

"He decided not to go to college after high school. After all, he knew everything. Besides, he would be a multimillionaire with his rock band before long; so a college degree wouldn't be necessary.

"Luke moved out on his own. Then, little by little, we saw glimpses of the invisible work God had been doing all along. Achieving the independence he had craved since birth caused Luke's relationship with us to improve. He asked his dad's advice, chatted about the Dodgers, and had real conversations with me.

"Little-by-little gave way to big-by-big. Luke devoured the Bible, attended church, and gave up bad habits. Since high school, every penny he made, all his hopes, dreams, goals, and time had centered around his band. The band members could scarcely wait to turn twenty-one so they could get gigs in bars and hit the big time. The day came, the gigs came, they were well received. Then God told Luke He wanted to do a new thing.

"This son of ours, who rarely had shared a personal thought or struggle since boyhood, asked his mom and dad to pray as he went to tell the band it was over. The band that played his original songs and for which he was the lead singer. Now, he was going to dash the other members' hopes and years of work because they 'weren't on the same page.'

"Now God has placed new songs on his lips, songs that bring glory to Him. He has emboldened the faith of moms in our group who are still waiting to see their sons and daughters turn wholeheartedly back to God."

Storming the Gates

I'm a mother just like Jan, just like you. I love my children just like you. I pray for them just like you. And, like so many mothers, I have travailed, wept, and stormed the gates of hell for the life of my prodigal.

At times I came before the Lord sobbing for his very life. Then feelings of unworthiness and failure as a mom would slip into my heart. The "if onlys" flooded my mind. How could God use me in ministry when my own family was struggling? How could I tell other moms that God would answer their prayers when I didn't see mine being answered? What would the women think when they heard about my son?

I needed God's strength, wisdom, unfailing love, and courage just to go about my normal activities as a wife, mother, and ministry leader. When I look back on those days, I can only say God's grace— His marvelous, matchless, wonderful grace—sustained me and kept me hoping and functioning.

I remember one day in particular I was feeling unworthy. Then I read Matthew 10:37–38: "Anyone who loves his father or mother more than me is not worthy of me; anyone who loves his son or daughter more than me is not worthy of me; and anyone who does not take his cross and follow me is not worthy of me."

The Holy Spirit stopped me on the phrase, "anyone who does not take his cross and follow me is not worthy of me." My only concern should be carrying my cross, being faithful to what God had called me to do. Even if it was hard. Even if I didn't understand. Even if I felt I couldn't go on.

I prayed, "Oh, Lord, I do love You more than my children, and I want to serve You until You take me home to dwell with You forever.

You're right. I can't carry my children's crosses. You will help them to carry theirs, just as You're helping me. What a relief to know that I'm only responsible for the cross that You have given me. That's all You ask of me. May I be found faithful."

I admire Billy Graham and his wife, Ruth, for being vulnerable concerning their prodigal son, Franklin. They diligently prayed for him and yet continued to serve the Lord. Billy Graham kept preaching in spite of his son's waywardness. Think of the thousands of people that might not have accepted Christ if Rev. Graham had quit preaching the gospel until his son got right with Jesus.

Persevering While Running

Like the Grahams, my task was to persevere in prayer for my children. With joy, I must run with perseverance the race God has marked out for me (Hebrews 12:1–2).

The following thoughts from *Streams in the Desert* ministered greatly to me as I tried to run the race with patience and to serve the Lord while grieving over my child.

> We commonly associate patience with laying down. We think of it as the angel that guards the couch of the invalid. Yet, I do not think the invalid's patience the hardest to achieve. There is a patience which I believe to be harder.... It is the power to *work* under a stroke; to have a great weight at your heart and still to run; to have a deep anguish in your spirit and still perform the daily task.... We are called to bury our sorrows not in lethargic quiescence, but in active service.... There is no burial of sorrow so difficult as that; it is the "*running* with patience."[5]

My children are now adults who each love the Lord. I can declare with John, "I have no greater joy than to hear that my children are walking in the truth" (3 John 4). How I praise God for helping me to keep to the task He had called me to. I would have missed out on so many blessings.

Dear Loving Father, I pray that the reader would experience Psalm 25:14 (AMP): "The secret [of the sweet, satisfying companionship] of the Lord have they who fear—revere and worship—Him, and He will show them His covenant, and reveal to them its [deep, inner] meaning."

Father, may Your words dwell richly in her. May she thirst for You as the deer pants for water. Help her each day to have quiet times with You. Give her assurance that You hear her cries and answer her prayers. May she know the joy of gathering with others to help carry their burdens through prayer. Bless her. Give her the courage, faith, and hope to continue steadfast in prayer—for every child needs a praying mom. Amen and amen.

Notes

1. Gary Bergel, "A Time for Prevailing Prayer," *Intercessors for America Newsletter,* Feb. 2001, 2.

2. Charles H. Spurgeon, *Morning and Evening,* (Grand Rapids, Mich.: Zondervan, 1980), Morning, Jan. 15.

3. Ron Hutchcraft, "Child Snatching," *A Word with You* #4123, *www.gospelcom.net.*

4. Wesley Duewel, *Mighty Prevailing Prayer,* (Grand Rapids, Mich.: Zondervan, 1990), 152.

5. Mrs. Charles E. Cowman, *Streams in the Desert,* (Grand Rapids Mich.: Zondervan, 1925), 314–15.

WHEN GOD

DOESN'T ANSWER

YOUR PRAYER

JERRY SITTSER

AUTHOR OF *A Grace Disguised*

I have always been drawn to the difficult questions of the Christian faith. For me perhaps the most troubling question of all is, "Why doesn't God answer our prayers?" This question is vexing because prayer is the one discipline in the Christian faith that makes us feel entirely dependent on God and thus sets us up for profound disappointment when God doesn't respond to our needs and requests.

The problem of unanswered prayer touches on a sensitive area, as if scratching a wound that refuses to heal. But it is on the minds of most praying people. We often turn to God at our most vulnerable moments, when all seems lost unless God steps in. Then why does he remain distant, silent, and hard when we call on him? If God doesn't respond when we need him most, then why pray at all?

Nevertheless, it is risky to take this issue on. I feel like I am standing on the edge of the Grand Canyon, staring into the abyss below. I am filled with both terror and wonder. I want to back away toward safety but remain frozen to the spot. I find myself compelled to ask hard questions about unanswered prayer because everything in me wants an answer and needs an answer. Still, I realize that the answer itself poses a threat. On the one hand, it might turn me away from God and undermine my desire to pray. On the other hand, it also might draw me deeper into God and engender in me even greater passion to pray.

I find that I am not alone. Most people I know have the same questions, feel the same vexation, and stand on the edge of the same abyss. If you are one of those people, I invite you to join me as we explore this mystery together.

Jerry Sittser

Unanswered Prayer
as a Gift

*I have lived to thank God that all
my prayers have not been answered.*
Jean Ingelow

IT IS EVERY MOTHER'S WORST NIGHTMARE.

She is the mother of a little boy, Kostya, who is only three years old. Kostya is dying of an incurable disease. The mother believes in God, and she believes that God can heal her little boy. She alternates agonizingly between hope and despair, fighting and giving up. Still, she prays, "imbuing her prayer with all the power of her soul, although somewhere deep within her she feared that God would not move the mountain—that he would act not according to her desires, but according to his own will."[1]

Her little boy dies. "Why," she thinks to herself, "why would the God to whom I prayed so much allow him to die? Why? Did my boy bother anyone? Did he do anything bad to anybody? Doesn't God know that he was my whole life, that I can't live without him? And then to suddenly take and torture this helpless, innocent little creature and shatter my life and answer all my prayers with his lifeless eyes, with his cold, stiff body. . . . Why pray to God if he can do such terrible things?"[2]

Leo Tolstoy tells this woman's story in a short story entitled "Prayer," which he wrote after reading about a shipwreck in the United States in which many children died. Tolstoy wrote the story to explore the problem of unanswered prayer. I read the story only recently, when I was pondering the problem myself. I once thought that unanswered prayer was either the result of God's sovereign will, which functions like a trump card, making our prayers largely irrelevant, or the result of human failure, which makes our prayers unacceptable to God, however needy we are. In either case, the outcome is the same—unanswered prayer.

A Startling Idea

Tolstoy put me onto a new idea, both troubling and helpful. *What would happen,* I wondered, *if all our prayers were answered?*

I searched my memory, trying to recall some of the prayers I prayed many years ago. I thought about the early and heady years of serving as a youth pastor in southern California when I was ready to conquer the world, with or without Christ. Though the church at which I served was healthy and growing, the youth program I inherited was a wreck. I realized at once that I faced an enormous challenge, just the kind of problem that made my blood run. I recruited several volunteers my own age who were as outrageous and audacious as I was. We abolished the old program, waited three months, and then started a new program called FUDD (Fishermen's Union of Dedicated Disciples). The new program struck us as cool as surfing at Huntington Beach.

We faced immediate resistance. Some parents were concerned about the demands we were putting on the kids, and some kids didn't like the emphasis on outreach. Parents complained; kids dropped out. We prayed with boldness and passion that God would bless our work. After nine months of hard and fruitless labor, we held a weekend retreat in the mountains. Forty-five students attended, a huge number to us. The weekend was electric, the quintessential mountaintop experience. Perhaps twenty students became Christians that weekend; many others experienced renewal. The momentum of that retreat continued for a long time. Within two years the high school group grew from twenty members to 125. It was *the* group in the area to attend. I was riding a wave of success. I witnessed many answers to prayer and enjoyed the fruits of my labor. Everything I touched turned into gold.

Eventually the ministry leveled off and lost momentum. And thank God it did, for I had become insufferably proud, a self-appointed expert in youth ministry. I wonder what would have happened to me had all my prayers been answered during those early years of ministry, if our group had continued to grow, if our program had continued to receive recognition. Perhaps unanswered prayer was good for me.

In his short story Tolstoy introduces a character, Mary, who is a nurse's aide and also an angel. Mary provides a divine perspective on the mother's loss. Could it be, Tolstoy asks, that unanswered prayer serves our own best interest? Instead of looking at unanswered prayer as the problem, Tolstoy explores whether *answered* prayer might be the problem. Could it be that unanswered prayer is a strange kind of gift?

That we pray does not in and of itself make us saints, for our prayers are often imbued with selfishness. When we pray, we pray not only as saints but also as sinners, very much inclined to use prayer to advance our own selfish interests, even when we pray out of desperation. Prayer for that reason is highly complex. On the one hand, the very act of praying reminds us that we are children of God. On the other hand, that same act of praying exposes us for the fallen creatures we are. As strange as it may sound, answered prayer could actually exacerbate the very problem in us—namely, sin—that God has acted in Jesus Christ to remedy, like a new medication that produces side-effects worse than the disease itself.

Thus, some prayers God won't or can't answer, for our own good. To answer these kinds of prayers would be bad for us and unworthy of God. We should never forget, especially when we pray, that we are sinful, fallible creatures, utterly dependent on God for life and salvation. When we pray, we should never forget the vast difference between God and us.

There is something in us, however, that causes us to forget. It is our pride, which, as the worst of the deadly sins, insidiously hides behind behaviors that appear as good, even religious practice. Pride tempts all of us to use prayer for base purposes. When we pray, therefore, we angle for things that would not be good for us or pleasing to God, even when we pray out of genuine neediness. Ironically, pride will take answers to our most desperate prayers and exploit them for some unworthy purpose.

Our prideful prayers put God into a dilemma — if he fails to answer our prayers, God appears mean and distant; if he answers our prayers, we end up worse off than before.

Our prideful prayers put God into a dilemma—if he fails to answer our prayers, God appears mean and distant; if he answers our prayers, we end up worse off than before.

WINNERS AND LOSERS

Prayer reinforces pride in at least two situations. The first occurs when we pray for victory at someone else's expense. Such prayers strive to make us winners and our opponents losers. We thus force God to take sides in a contest or dispute or conflict we want to win, at all costs. As Mary says to the distraught mother in Tolstoy's short story, "You should not be angry with God. He cannot listen to everyone. Sometimes people hear only one side, and in order to do good for one the other is abused."[3]

But what if people from the other side are praying for victory, too? If two people pray for opposite things, then God cannot answer both prayers at the same time. The requests are mutually exclusive.

If God answered both, then he would contradict himself. So one person at least—and perhaps both—will be disappointed because God doesn't answer her or their prayers. It could be that God doesn't take sides at all, at least not in the way we would like.

Perhaps the people who attribute victory to God are giving God credit for something he didn't do. In situations involving a win or a loss, God might actually stand on the side of those who lose. He might be eager to answer their prayers because his ear is turned toward the cry of the weak and desperate. Besides, it could be that the loss propelled them to pray for what matters most in God's eyes—humility, courage, and patience. We must beware, in other words, of assuming that God is on our side when we win and not on the side of those who lose, as if victory implies God's favor and loss means God's rejection. Then again, we must be equally cautious about assuming that, because God takes the side of those who lose, he always opposes those who win. Perhaps God doesn't think in terms of losing or winning at all, at least not in the way we are inclined to.

When my oldest son, David, was in elementary school, he played on a soccer team that dominated the city league. At one point his team won twenty straight matches, culminating in a victory in the city tournament at season's end. But during the following year David's team lost four matches in a row, including one lopsided loss to a team that had never beaten them. That team gloated and taunted David and his teammates after the match, which only made matters worse.

David's team rallied during the final city tournament, however, playing well enough to make it into the finals. To their dismay, they had to square off against the team that had beaten them so badly only a few weeks before. Both teams played well. At the end of regulation play, the score was tied two to two. So the teams had to go into a shoot-out. A shoot-out requires five players from each team to shoot against the opposing goalkeeper from twelve yards out. Whichever team scores the most goals in the shootout wins the match.

By this time the parents on our side had turned the match into something akin to a medieval crusade, complete with all the spiritual overtones. I heard several parents mutter, "Please, Lord, let our boys win." One woman said, "God, if they win, I will believe in you again." Not to be outdone, I—a seasoned Christian, an ordained minister, an author of books on theology, a professor with a Ph.D.—joined this chorus of prayer and even conjured up several reasons why God should answer our prayers.

Our team won when our goalkeeper blocked the last shot. The kids went wild, leaping into the air and piling on top of each other. It looked like a scene from a Disney movie. One parent said, "I believe there's a God again." Being more modest and pious, I simply uttered a prayer of thanksgiving under my breath.

We had no way of knowing, of course, what was happening on the other side of the field. I learned more about the other team only recently, some five years later, when I met a Christian parent from the opposing side. In the course of our conversation she described a tournament in which her son had played years earlier. At first I had no idea that she was talking about the famous match.

Her son's team, she reported, had suffered a "devastating" loss in the finals. As she described it, their team had been a perennial loser, especially to one particular team that had "no idea what it felt like to lose." Their team had finally beaten this nemesis, and badly, too. They had to face the same team again in the tournament finals. Their team "needed" that victory, she said, to add the finishing touches to the only winning season they had ever had. But they lost—"in a shootout," she said, "and on the last shot." Only then did I realize that she was talking about the same match.

Did God answer our prayers and deny theirs? I don't think so. For all I know, God answered their prayers in a more significant way. Perhaps they had been praying that their sons would grow up well, learning to honor God, to become people of character, and to develop perspective in life so that winning or losing a soccer match would become less and less important. Adversity, after all, probably does more to help people grow up than easy victories. In the end losing might have been better for them than winning was for us.

As I look back now, I think that our prayers were silly, short-sighted, and selfish. But is that really surprising? We often say self-ish prayers without thinking much about them. We pray for parking spaces when we're running late, never considering that ten other people, as late as we are, might be praying, too, for the two remaining spaces available in the parking garage. We pray for victories in elections, forgetting that victory for one party means defeat for another party that might be just as prayerful as we are. We pray for success in business, though increased sales in our business might undermine competitors down the street who are praying for the same thing and need success more than we do. Not that these prayers are necessarily wrong, but we should remember that answers to our prayers might be at someone else's expense.

These are innocent examples. But not every case is so innocent. Sometimes people pray for victory when the stakes are high and prayer seems like the only alternative to despair and defeat. Christians on opposing sides have prayed for victory in conflicts that were—and are—far more serious and deadly. Some Christians in the United States are praying for Israel's victory over the Palestinians, while Christians in Palestine are praying not for victory but for peace. Again, some Christians in Northern Ireland are praying for the defeat of "the enemy," whether Protestant or Catholic, while other Christians are praying not for vindication but for rec-onciliation. And some Christians in the United States are praying for the prosperity of our nation, while Christians in other parts of the world are praying for enough food to survive another day.

The same problem occurred during the Civil War. Both North and South claimed that God was on their side, quoted from the same Bible but came to opposite conclusions, and prayed for victory over their fellow countrymen. Obviously, God could not answer every one of their prayers.

Ironically, Abraham Lincoln, the only president who never joined a church (though he did attend a Presbyterian church) and who was often accused of being irreligious, expressed probably the most profound theological analysis of the war. While Christians from both sides claimed that God was on their side, Lincoln wondered whether God was on either side. "Both [sides] read the same Bible, and pray to the same God; and each invokes His aid against the other. It may seem strange that any man should dare to ask a just God's assistance in wringing their bread from the sweat of other men's faces. . . . The prayers of both could not be answered; that of neither has been answered fully. The Almighty has His own purposes."

We pray for victory, as does the other side. But how do we know that we are right and the other side wrong? Even if we are right—clearly there are occasions when one side is right and the other side is wrong!—God may still have a purpose in mind that transcends our own. Besides, it is possible to be perfectly right on a superficial level and yet wrong in the things that matter most in life. At the least, then, we must be humble when we pray, recognizing that God is sovereign. Though victory for one side may be good and right, that victory may still play a small role in a much bigger plan God is working out. God may takes sides, but not necessarily our side, even if, as is sometimes the case, we are actually right.

That is the danger of praying for victory. Our cause may be right, in a narrow sense. But we may still be wrong in a larger sense—manifesting pride, gloating in victory, punishing wrongdo-ers with excessive severity, and excusing sin. The great hazard for people on a crusade is that, however legitimate the crusade, they become blind to their own faults. So confident are they of being right and of having God on their side that they lose the capacity to discover that they may be wrong, too. They oppose abortion but don't care about the needs of women. They fight for civil rights but treat secretaries and janitors like second-class citizens. They uphold the standards of biblical sexuality but show little grace toward their spouses and children.

So when we pray for victory, as sometimes we must, we should always, always pray with humility. Otherwise the "victories" we gain will be Pyrrhic only, won at too great a cost. What does it profit, asks Jesus, if we gain the whole world—winning every conflict in which we are engaged—but lose our own soul?

POWER AT TOO HIGH A COST

Thus praying for victory at someone else's expense is the first occasion when our prayers might not be answered. The second occasion occurs when answers to prayer would lead to our spiritual ruin. Again, I have only recently wrestled with this problem.

I have known for many years that power is dangerous, even for those who seem to have a good reason to assert it. Both experience and history teach us this. Economic power (e.g., wealth) can make people materialistic and greedy; political power (elected office) can serve petty and selfish interests; intellectual power (academic posts) can capitulate to ideology and thus fail to search for truth; military power can bully and punish for wrongs, whether done or not done. History contains too many examples of power gone bad, ruining the people who had it. All forms of power are inherently dangerous.

We usually think ourselves to be the exception to the rule. I know I do. I am confident, in my self-delusion, that power would not corrupt me because I think I am nearly always right, very wise, and so capable of wielding it. So, if I had power, I would use it responsibly, never mind the failures of everyone else. It is easy to be altruistic in theory, when I am speculating about what I would do with power if I had it. It is hard to be altruistic in fact.

When we have no money, we say we would be generous if we had some; but then we find good reasons to spend money on ourselves when our income rises, which is why the least generous people (at least in terms of percentage of income given) are the rich. We claim that we will uphold the cause of justice before we enter politics; but then, once we assume office, we use the office to serve our own interests. We imagine ourselves courageously pursuing truth when we first enter the field of higher education; but by the time we have earned tenure, we are caught up in the latest intellectual fashion and conceit. We are almost completely incapable of using power for a greater good.

When Lynda and I were first married, we barely scraped by on my feeble income. We had to pinch pennies to contribute a tithe to the church. Now, years later, my income is far greater. I have enough money for both needs and wants, with some left over. Yet I find it harder now to give than I did years ago, when I lived in virtual poverty. More money has not made me more generous, at least not in my heart.

I am also a full professor, having progressed through the various ranks until I can rise no further. I used to ponder what it would be like to hold the highest rank at the college. I imagined giving generously of my time to the college, volunteering for administrative tasks and mentoring new colleagues. Yet I am more jealous of my time now, more wary of taking on projects that do not serve my own scholarly interests, and more protective of programs and courses I have developed. I have to force myself to share the power I have, to make room for new blood and new ideas.

THE DANGER OF SPIRITUAL POWER

Surprisingly, spiritual power can be as dangerous as any other kind of power. The primary means of access to spiritual power, of course, is prayer. When we pray, we call upon a transcendent God to use his power to perform some good deed—to heal a loved one who is sick, to give us wisdom when making a decision, to prosper a new ministry, to defend the cause of justice, to give us influence in the world. For a long time I did not recognize the danger of spiritual power. It hadn't occurred to me that spiritual power, the power we access through prayer, is as corruptible as any other form of power, if not more so.

Perhaps no writer in the twentieth century has explored the corrosive nature of power, including spiritual power, more than J. R. R. Tolkien, author of the famous *The Lord of the Rings* trilogy. Tolkien did not write the trilogy in a vacuum. He had experienced the ravages of two world wars. The first war in particular, fought between supposedly Christian empires, exacted a huge toll in human life (ten million dead) and raised haunting questions in his mind about power.

Tolkien wrote the trilogy to explore this theme, among others. Sauron, an evil sorcerer, forges twenty magical rings—three for the elves, seven for the dwarves, and nine for human kings. But he keeps one for himself, and this ring, "the one to rule them all and in the darkness bind them," is the most powerful of all. It controls the others.

This ring serves as a metaphor for supernatural power. No matter how well intentioned, the person who possesses this one ring will eventually use it for evil purposes. There appears to be no exceptions to that rule. So the best among them—Gandalf the wizard, Galadriel the elven queen, and Aragorn the true king—simply refuse to seize the ring, though they have chances, because they recognize their own weakness and their susceptibility to corruption. They choose to live in weakness and humility, even to suffer defeat if they must, rather than risk the corruption that the power of the ring would cause.

Still, the temptation they face to use the power of the ring, even for a supposedly good purpose, is almost too much to overcome. What tempts the best among them, like Gandalf, is the desire to use the ring to accomplish good. It is power for the sake of showing pity that becomes the real danger because, however well intentioned, the power of the ring would still worm its way into the heart and turn it toward evil. At one point Frodo, a Hobbit and keeper of the ring, says to Gandalf, a great and good wizard, "You are wise and powerful. Will you not take the Ring?" Gandalf replies:

> "No! With that power I should have power too great and terrible. And over me the Ring would gain a power still greater and more deadly. . . . Yet the way of the Ring to my heart is by pity, pity for weakness and the desire of strength to do good. Do not tempt me! I dare not take it, not even to keep it safe, unused. The wish to wield it would be too great for my strength."[4]

Ironically, it is Frodo, the "Halfling," a creature who has no ambition for greatness and wants nothing more than to live a quiet, peaceable life, who is commissioned to take the Ring to Mount Doom in the land of Mordor, where it can be destroyed. Frodo is humble and powerless, which qualifies him to carry out the mission because he is the least likely to use the power of the Ring, even to help others.

I am not suggesting that prayer is like that ring, inherently evil. Frodo was commissioned to destroy the ring because it was corrupt, however good the motives of those who tried to use it. It is hardly the case that prayer is corrupt in the same way. Still, there is something dangerous about prayer. Or better to say, there is something dangerous about us once we receive answers to prayer. God answers prayer for our own good and for his glory. But what we could do with those answers to prayer might turn into something quite different.

Spiritual power is greater than all other kinds of power because it comes directly from God. It is mightier than armies and education and office and wealth. It is the power that created the world, that sustains the world, that redeems the world. It is the power that can heal the blind and raise people from the dead. It is the power that can transform the human heart. There is no power as wonderful and good as spiritual power. It is for that very reason that it is so terrible and dangerous, not because of what God does with it but because of what we might do. God is merciful to us when he does not grant us such power on a whim or wish.

THE ABUSIVE POWER OF PRAYER

Like all other means to power, prayer too is subject to abuse. Our prayers can become selfish and mean and petty. God therefore shows us mercy by not answering all our prayers. If God did answer all our prayers, we would become corrupt beyond measure, praying as if prayer was like a credit card with no limits. We claim, of course, that we would use it for a good purpose and thus pray for noble things.

We can make such a claim because it is only that—a claim, an ideal, a theoretical assertion. It is easy to boast of what our prayers would accomplish when so many of our prayers accomplish little or nothing.

But if our prayers were answered—not some of them but *all* of them, especially our very best and worthiest prayers—we would become monsters, far worse than Hitler or Stalin. At first we would be silly, like a little boy showing off a new toy that's the envy of the neighborhood. We would make trees fly in the air, drive our Volvos across the Mississippi, and turn the moon into green cheese.

Then we would become more serious, even noble. The exigencies of life would force us to it. We would pray to God because we had nowhere else to turn and no one else to turn to. We would pray for something we desperately needed or wanted, knowing that an answer from God was our last option. We would pray as I did, so many years ago, asking God to spare the lives of my broken and dying family members after that horrible accident.

What if God had answered that prayer for healing, perhaps the most sincere and desperate prayer I have ever prayed? What if God had instantaneously healed my wife, Lynda, my daughter Diana Jane, and my mother, Grace, right on the spot, dazzling everyone—not only the witnesses on the scene but also everyone else who would hear about it? What would have happened? I can only speculate.

Certainly people would have been shocked and curious. The incident would have received attention from around the world. Newspapers would have covered it for days. Photos of my family would have appeared on the cover of major magazines, and television news programs and talk shows would have clamored to interview us. We would have been given incredible opportunities to witness to our faith and to glorify God.

Perhaps I would have been motivated to do nothing more than to help others and to honor God, at least initially. Perhaps my ministry would have started out that innocently. But it would not have stayed that way for long. Eventually I would have become an expert on prayer and a medium of the miraculous between God and everyone else. I would have been forced to hire an agent and a staff. I would have written a book on prayer (with a very different title from the title of this book!), attracted a following, and started an organization called "Miracle Ministries." I would have held prayer crusades around the world, helping people tap into God's healing power. I would have become famous, powerful, and rich.

Isn't this how it usually works? Isn't this how corruption takes root? God does something extraordinary, like healing family members catastrophically injured in an accident. We want others to experience the same blessing. So we market the miraculous, turn prayer into a technique anyone can master, and win the acclaim of the world. Am I being cynical about human nature? Some programs on religious television remind me that my sober analysis of human nature is not far from the mark.

If God answered all our prayers, sooner or later we would use prayer to advance our own interests and to win the world's acclaim. We would become, as James warned, "a friend of the world" and thus "an enemy of God."[5] We would use the power of prayer simply to gain more power for ourselves until only God stood in our way.

And then we would challenge even God. We would become like the devil himself—pompous, proud, and audacious—using prayer as a means of exalting ourselves, showing off, and taking God's place. Isn't that what Adam and Eve tried to do before they were driven out of the Garden of Eden? Isn't that what the devil tried to do before he was driven out of heaven?

In short, we would use the power of prayer for our own benefit (such as health and wealth, success, and domination) rather than for the good things God wants for us (such as holiness of life, faithfulness in service, and goodness of heart)—even if our initial prayers were desperate and our initial intentions innocent. This all sounds fanciful, I know. But it is not. It is no joking matter. We think we would be exceptions to the rule. But such would never be the case. Spiritual power would intoxicate and corrupt us. The results would be disastrous.

Protection from Ourselves

Is there any exception to the rule? I can think of only one. Jesus himself was aware of the danger of spiritual power. Of all people who could have justified having and using spiritual power, Jesus was surely the one. He waited thirty years before his ministry commenced. His life during those years was so ordinary that we know little about it. There was nothing much to report. He worked as a carpenter, perhaps helped to raise his younger siblings, and meditated on the Torah.

Those years of responsibility, solitude, and obscurity prepared him for the three short years of his public ministry. He began that ministry shortly after John baptized him, the Holy Spirit descended upon him, and his Father in heaven affirmed him as his Son. One would think that Jesus was ready for service by then; he had been seasoned, baptized, affirmed, and filled.

But first he had to face temptation. So the Holy Spirit drove Jesus into the desert, where he was tempted by the devil. Three times the devil tempted Jesus to abuse spiritual power—to indulge his appetites by turning a stone into bread, to gain power over the world by bowing down to the god of this world, and to impress people by performing a miracle, thus winning their admiration. Jesus had all the reason in the world to yield to these temptations. He was hungry. Why not indulge his appetite? Jesus was heir apparent to the world's throne. Why not take a shortcut and feign allegiance to the devil? Jesus was going to be a miracle-worker anyway. Why not dazzle the crowds, making it easier for them to believe?

But Jesus resisted. It was the wrong place, the wrong time, the wrong circumstances to claim and use such power. What qualified Jesus to use spiritual power so effectively is that he put it aside, refusing to use it to advance his own interests. He chose to suffer deprivation first, allowing himself to be purged and purified and thus prepared for the power he would use after he passed the tests.

Ironically, later on Jesus did receive power, prayed fervently, and exercised tremendous influence. He multiplied five loaves and two fishes to feed five thousand people, after having prayed to his Father in heaven. He performed countless miracles—to show mercy, not to show off. Now he is Lord of the entire universe, though only after facing humiliation, suffering, and death. He refused to take advantage of a power that was rightfully his and to assert himself, though he had every right to. Paul states it so well. "Though [Jesus] was in the form of God, he did not regard equality with God as something to be exploited, but emptied himself, taking the form of a slave, being born in human likeness. And being found in human form, he humbled himself and became obedient to the point of death—even death on a cross."[6]

That commitment to humility and sacrifice continued to the end, even though Jesus himself seemed at one point to waver, for an obviously understandable reason. Who wouldn't shrink in utter terror at the thought of such an ignominious death? In the Garden of Gethsemane Jesus prayed, "My Father, if it is possible, may this cup be taken from me." That was his prayer, though he added, "yet not as I will, but as you will."[7] Obviously his prayer was not answered—for our sake, not for his. Imagine if Jesus' prayer had been answered! His life would have been spared, ours doomed. Jesus deserved to have his prayer answered, too. God was merciful, not to Jesus but to us, by refusing to answer the prayer of his own perfect and innocent Son.

We are not dealing here with conventional mathematics applied to the spiritual life. According to the Bible, death leads to life, loss to gain, weakness to strength, and suffering to power. Unanswered prayer breaks us, seasons us, and refines us so that, in the end, we attain greater spiritual depth and greater spiritual power.

I am reminded once again of another line in Tolstoy's short story, "Prayer." Mary explains to the mother who has just lost her son:

> "Sometimes it happens like this: Without being guilty of any-
> thing, a family can become bankrupt, lose their business, and,
> instead of a good apartment, live in some dirty room. They
> don't even have money to buy tea! They all weep, praying for

some kind of help. God could satisfy all of their prayers, but he knows that it wouldn't be good for them. They don't see it, but the Father knows that if they lived in luxury with lots of money, they would become completely spoiled."[8]

Hannah Whitall Smith, a nineteenth-century Quaker born and raised in the United States, faced much suffering in her life, though she was an extraordinary woman of influence and prayer. Smith lost four of her seven children. Later, after moving to England, she had to raise two of her grandchildren as well. In her old age she was disabled with rheumatism and spent time in a wheelchair. Yet she relished life, enjoyed God, and loved the people around her. Her grandchildren in particular remembered her romping with them with unbridled enthusiasm. She shared her insights about the Christian faith in *The Christian's Secret of a Happy Life*, which, in addition to imparting practical wisdom about Christian living, contains many prayers.

Unanswered prayer breaks us, seasons us, and refines us so that, in the end, we attain greater spiritual depth and greater spiritual power.

The unanswered prayers resulting in suffering did not turn Smith away from prayer; it drove her deeper into prayer. "It has been well said that 'earthly cares are a heavenly discipline.' But they are even something better than discipline—they are God's chariots, sent to take the soul to its high places of triumph. They do not look like chariots. They look instead like enemies, sufferings, trials, defeats, misunderstandings, disappointments, unkindness."[9]

Strange as it may sound, we need unanswered prayer. It is God's gift to us because it protects us from ourselves. If all our prayers were answered, we would only abuse the power. We would use prayer to change the world to our liking, and it would become hell on earth. Like spoiled children with too many toys and too much money, we would only grab for more. We would pray for victory at the expense of others; we would be intoxicated by the power we would wield. We would hurt other people and exalt ourselves.

Strange as it may sound, we need unanswered prayer. It is God's gift to us because it protects us from ourselves.

Unanswered prayer protects us. It breaks us, deepens us, exposes us, and transforms us. Ironically, the unanswered prayers of the past, which so often leave us feeling hurt, abandoned, and disillusioned, serve as a refiner's fire that prepares us for the answered prayers of the future, if we are willing to look deep into the darkness of our own souls and persist in prayer when there doesn't seem to be any reason to.

QUESTIONS FOR DISCUSSION

1. Think of some examples from your past in which it was good that a prayer was *not* answered.

2. Explore the reasons why prayer for victory can be justifiable. Consider when such prayers might still be wrong. Cite some examples.

3. How can the power of prayer be a dangerous thing? Give some examples.

4. Why were the temptations Jesus faced in the desert so dangerous? How did he resist them?

5. Reflect on the occasions when unanswered prayer ended up being a gift to you.

NOTES

1. Leo Tolstoy, "Prayer," *Divine and Human* (Grand Rapids: Zondervan, 2000), 40.

2. Ibid., 41.

3. Ibid., 41.

4. J. R. R. Tolkein, *The Fellowship of the Ring: The Lord of the Rings* (New York: Houghton, Mifflin, & Co., 1954), 60.

5. See James 4:4.

6. Philippians 2:6–8 (NRSV).

7. Matthew 26:39.

8. Leo Tolstoy, "Prayer," 42.

9. Hannah Whitall Smith, *The Christian Secret of a Happy Life* (Old Tappan, N.J.: Spire Books, 1970), 159–60.

DR. HENRY CLOUD
DR. JOHN TOWNSEND

Authors of the Million-Copy Best-Seller BOUNDARIES

BOUNDARIES
FACE TO FACE

HOW TO HAVE THAT
DIFFICULT CONVERSATION
YOU'VE BEEN AVOIDING

Successful people confront well. They know that setting healthy boundaries improves relationships. They have discovered that uncomfortable—even dangerous—situations can often be avoided or resolved through direct conversation. But most of us don't know how to go about having difficult conversations. We see confrontation as scary or adversarial. We're afraid to ask a boss for a raise or talk to a relative about a drinking problem, or even address a relational conflict with a spouse or someone we are dating.

It is our hope that *Boundaries Face to Face* will help you understand why confrontation is essential in all areas of life. The book will let you see how healthy confrontation can improve relationships, demonstrate the essentials of a good boundary-setting conversation, and provide tips to help prepare for the conversation.

As you enjoy the excerpted chapter "Asking for What You Want," we hope you will realize you can stop bad behavior and know how to deal with counterattack in that difficult conversation you have been avoiding.

Drs. Henry Cloud and John Townsend

●●●

CHAPTER 17

Asking for
What You Want

Peter was sad over his recent breakup with Jan. He really liked her spunk, energy, and passion for life, and at one point even thought they might marry. I had thought she might be the "one" for him as well, so I was surprised when he told me he had broken up with her.

"What happened?" I (Henry) asked.

"I just couldn't deal with her demandingness," he said. "She wanted everything her way, and she was so pushy. I thought about a lifetime of that and got a headache thinking about it. I know I liked her, but in the end, she was just too much."

I understood what he meant, because I thought she was pushy too. I remember thinking that if he married her, he would be a very busy boy. She made you feel that you needed to dig in. But I felt for him in the split up. He was sad and would miss her.

Not too long after that, he began dating Marla. At first, he was in absolute heaven. She was so "easy to get along with, not like Jan at all," he said. "She is not pushy; she's up and positive so much of the time. It feels like I have emerged from winter."

About five months later, something happened. "I broke up with Marla," he said. "It just wasn't working out."

"What happened?" I asked. "I thought she was the answer to all of your 'woman' issues. Not demanding, not pushy, not controlling. You were so into her."

"I know. It's weird! In the beginning I really liked that she was not like Jan, always wanting something and so demanding. She was like a breath of fresh air. But as time went on, I noticed a couple of things. First, I could never figure out what she wanted. I would ask her what she wanted to do, or where she wanted to go, or how she felt about something, and she would always defer to me. Even though that felt good in the beginning, I think I was just gun-shy from Jan. Over time, I got bored with Marla's flexibility. There was something missing. I don't know exactly what it was. Second, I started to see another part of her that drove me a little batty."

"What was that?"

"I don't know the right word for it. *Pouty* is a little strong. She wouldn't really pout, but she would be sad, or quiet, or something. I would feel like I had done something wrong, but I didn't know what it was. So I would ask. At first, she would say, 'Nothing,' but I knew that was bull. So I would have to pull it out of her, and then I would find out that she had wanted me to do something I hadn't done, or that she was bugged about something she hadn't told me about. I felt like I was letting her down, but I couldn't read her mind. I was frustrated not knowing when things were okay and when they weren't. I think I need someone more up front with what they are thinking and what they want."

"Like Jan?" I asked.

"Oh, no!" he said, startled. "Maybe, but no. No. I don't really know." He looked confused and a little sad. At that moment he didn't have a lot of hope for a good relationship.

Wanting Well

Peter's problem is not hard to understand. He wanted a woman with passion and desire, but he didn't want to be controlled by her. He wanted to give freely, but he didn't want to have to figure out what someone wants.

As I told Peter later, he *wanted someone who wanted* well. On the one hand, Jan wanted strongly, and he liked that, but she expressed her desires in a way that ultimately drove him away. She did not want well, or at least communicate her wants and desires well. On the other hand, Marla wanted weakly; her wants were almost invisible, until Peter didn't meet them. Only after disappointing her did he know what they were. Jan's and Marla's inability to communicate their wants left Peter looking for something else.

Sadly, Peter probably could have worked it out with either Jan or Marla had he understood at that time what the issue was. Committed married people do that all the time. And later he did figure it out with another woman. But married or single, in romance, family life, friendship, or business relationships, many people can identify with the problem of getting what they want in their relationships in a way that is good for both parties. How do you communicate wants in a way that gets your desires met and doesn't drive someone away? That's the topic of this chapter.

You Can't Always Get What You Want, But You'd Better Try

Solomon said it well: "Hope deferred makes the heart sick, but a longing fulfilled is a tree of life" (Prov. 13:12).

Your heart's desires and longings bring life to your life. If you don't have ways of making them known, they won't be met, and you'll feel "sick at heart." Wanting is key to feeling alive in a relationship, key to keeping the relationship vibrant for both people. If only one person is getting his or her desires met, the relationship suffers, intimacy lessens, and sickness of heart results.

Unfortunately, many people do not get what they want in relationships where they could if they knew how to communicate their desires. Jan had that problem, and ultimately she lost what she wanted. Marla had the same problem in a different way. And although he didn't know it, Peter did too. Had he been able to tell either Jan or Marla what he wanted from them, things might have turned out different. Instead, he just reacted to them, and left.

Wanting is difficult, in the best of scenarios. Many things can get in the way. But in the end, wanting is the only way to live fully, and if that is true, then we need to learn how to communicate our wants in ways best for us and best for our relationships. Let's look at some ways to do that, some ways not to, and how to handle what can happen when we want well.

Know Whose Want It Is and Who Is Responsible for It

Many people, when they think of "boundaries," think of them only as setting limits, saying no, or trying to stop something destructive from happening. But having good boundaries is more than stopping bad things from happening to you. *It is also taking responsibility for the good things you want to happen.*

When you take responsibility for your desires and communicate them well, a relationship has much more chemistry, connection, and mutual fulfillment. You know about and negotiate any issues; there is give and take. And no one is walking around resentful and depressed.

Think about Marla for a moment. She had desires she wanted fulfilled in her relationship with Peter. But she thought Peter was responsible for knowing what her desires were and for taking the first step toward fulfilling them. She shifted the responsibility for what she wanted from her to him; she thought her "wants" were his problem, not hers. When he did not solve her problem, when she felt sad or resentful, she saw it as Peter's responsibility to figure out what she was feeling and do something about it. Ultimately, this proved too much for him to do.

To have a relationship that works well, Marla first needs to communicate her wants not outwardly, but inwardly. She needs to have a "responsibility" talk with herself before she has a "talk" with another person. Here are some of the things she will need to do:

- Own her "want"—be honest with herself about what she wants and be aware that her desire is her responsibility

- Own the feelings that occur when her desire is not getting met—if she is sad, she needs to tell Peter, not wait for him to figure it out
- Choose to communicate and move toward Peter to let her wants be known
- Communicate desire, not demand

If Marla approaches the process this way, she will be off to a much better start. She will be getting "the log out of her own eye" first. We always have to look at ourselves first to make sure we are doing our part correctly. This is particularly true with wants and desires; others do not magically know what we want, and they need to be told in ways they can accept. So the first conversation has to take place inside. Here is how the conversation would sound inside the old Marla and then inside the new one:

The Old Marla: I want to go to see a good thought-provoking movie tonight. I don't want to see another action movie. Peter always chooses those. I wish he would be more considerate and do what I want for once. I hope that happens, but it probably won't. He knows I like deeper movies, so maybe for once, he'll ask me. I doubt it. I'm bummed. He isn't going to do that. I don't know why I even hope for it. This feels really crummy.

The New Marla: I want to go to a good thought-provoking movie tonight. I bet Peter is thinking about another action movie. If I don't say something, I'll end up being bummed out again. I'll end the evening in a crummy mood and want to eat five gallons of ice cream. It would be nice if he asked me what I want to see, but I doubt he will. I'd better call him to let him know what I'm thinking. Wait, what if he doesn't want to see a thought-provoking movie? Well, we'll just talk about it. I'll tell him the movies I want to see, and I'll ask him what he wants to see. That's fair. Oh well, if he doesn't want to see one of the movies I want to see, I'll deal with it then. He's free to say no. It won't be the end of the world. Maybe I'll go with Jill if Peter doesn't want to go. I'll see how it goes.

The big difference between these two internal dialogues is that in the second one, Marla is taking ownership of her desire. She is thinking of how to actively communicate what she wants to Peter. It starts with how she handles her desire inside of herself long before she gets to the conversation with Peter. It starts with her realizing that her desires are her responsibility.

Preserve the Other Person's Freedom

Ask yourself this question: "What do I do when I hear no to something I want?" Here are some not-so-good reactions:

- I get mad, either inwardly or outwardly. I have an internal or external temper tantrum.
- I judge the other person, thinking that she "should" do what I ask; I think she is selfish or doesn't care about me.
- I go further than judging. I see the other person as really bad; I don't see him as good at all. All I see is bad.
- I emotionally or physically withdraw from the person.
- I feel hurt and unloved.
- I try to make her feel guilty, either to punish her or to get her to do what I want.
- I become cynical about ever getting what I want in life or the relationship.
- I turn into a judge, prosecutor, and salesperson. I object to every reason he has for saying no.
- I smile on the outside and hide my real feelings, going along as if it's okay when it's not.

Freedom is essential to a good relationship. If we're not free, we can't love. If people feel that they can't say no to us and if they do things for us out of compulsion, guilt, or feelings of obligation, they will resent doing those things. Freedom and love suffer, and even fulfilled desires can't fully fulfill because they are not given in love.

There are no magic words to show someone they are free to say no, other than telling them. Here are some suggestions on how to do that:

"I don't want you to feel like you 'have to' do this, but could you give me a ride to work tomorrow?"

"I want you to feel totally free to not do this, so tell me if you don't want to. Will you help me move this weekend?"

"I don't want you to feel any pressure about this, so I want you to know that going in. Feel free to tell me no, okay? So here it is—I want you to join this committee with me and help me organize the Fall Festival."

People who find it difficult to ask for things may find it helpful to say things like this to put the other person at ease. If you have controlled someone in the past or have been demanding, or even if that person *feels as if you have*, you may want to preface your request with statements like this to remind the person that he or she can say no to you now.

Another way to preserve another person's freedom is to avoid the word *need* when it is not accurate. A "need" is something we must have for survival. If we do not have what we need, we suffer injury. We *need* air, water, food, safety, and connection. It is rare that only one person can provide something we need. Most of the time we are talking about "wants," not "needs." When we use the word *need*, it smells more like an obligation than a request. Who feels free to say no to someone's request for air, water, or food? So when you are talking about what you *want* from someone, beware of casting it in terms of a *need*.

When a relationship becomes close, the stakes go up in terms of the distress one may feel when one doesn't get something. For example, if a woman is going to be intimate with a man, she needs to be able to trust him. But even then, she needs to talk about what she wants him to do. For example, here are two different ways of making the same request:

"I want to be close to you. And to be close, I need to feel like you are committed to me. So I would like you to spend one

of the weekend days with me and see your buddies on the
other day."

"I need for you to be with me on one of the weekend days. You
can't expect me to be close to you when you are gone both
days."

The first request expresses vulnerability; the second feels more like
a demand.

Communicating wants is very touchy, and the words we say are not
always the issue. The real issue may be the attitude we take when we
communicate our desires. So, no matter what you say, observe your attitude when you talk. Make your request in a way that shows you are
not implying that the other person "should" do whatever you want, but
instead shows that you realize you are not "entitled" to what you are
asking for. Don't remind the other person of all you have done for him
or her, or some other form of manipulation that communicates that
he or she "should" do what you ask.

Observe how you respond and react to another person's choices.
Don't punish or react. If he or she says no, don't come back with one
of the following rejoinders:

"Fine. Excuse me for wanting something."
"It seems like the least you could do."
"That will be the last time I ever ask *you* for anything."
"It seems like after all I have done for you, the least you could
do would be...."
"See? It doesn't do any good to ask you for what I want."

Look at your reactions and see how much freedom people really have
to say no to you.

Be Clear, and Be Direct

The best way to ask for what you want is to be clear and direct. Do
this by using "I" statements, not "you" statements:

"I" statement: "I would like it if we could talk more than we
have been doing. I would like to know more of what is going
on with you. I feel out of the loop."

"You" statement: "You don't ever really talk to me very much.
You leave me in total darkness. Seems like you would want
to tell me things if we were really close."

"You" statement: "It seems like you don't care, judging from
how much you talk to me."

The "I" statement is very clear and responsible. Talk about *you*, not
the other person and his or her failures to provide for you. The "you"
statements judge, interpret, and globalize. "You" statements accuse the
other person.

Be specific instead of global when expressing wants. When a husband says, "We never have any intimacy," he is not being specific. Here
is how he can be more direct in stating what he wants:

"I want to make love with you."

"I want to take a vacation with you."

"I want to take an afternoon and spend some time talking
about our goals together."

The use of "I" statements seems simple, but it is especially important
in communicating your wants and desires. Remember the slogan "Just
say no"? Well, the rule here is "Just say":

"I want to go out to eat tonight."

"I would like you to call if you are going to be late for dinner."

"I would like you to pick up your clothes off the bathroom
floor."

If you are going to use "you" statements, use them in requests, like
the above, instead of accusations:

"Would you please pick up the dry cleaning for me on the way
home?"

"Would you dance with me?"

"Will you be willing to take care of the kids so I can go out
with my friends?"

All of these requests preserve the freedom of the other person. They
do not bind the other person into some "no choice" position, and they
decrease the possibility of his or her becoming defensive.

What Can Happen, and What Do I Do Then?

When you ask for something, several things can happen. You can receive
an unqualified yes. A yes is not too difficult to deal with, unless you
have trouble receiving good things, but that is a different book! The
harder times are when you get a no, an objection, defensiveness, or a
personal attack just for asking.

In dealing with responses when you have asked for something,
remember the principles we talked about for asking. They also apply for
responding.

First, take ownership of your desire. It is your desire, not that of the
person who just said no.

Second, don't punish, retaliate, or use counterattack. Try one of
the following alternatives.

1. Accept the No and Move On

One of the biggest problems with the "Jans" of the world is that no
"no" is acceptable to them. Peter felt as though if he did not do whatever Jan wanted, he was going to be in trouble. So make sure you do not
have a "have to have" attitude about everything you ask for, and don't
see a no as something bad. After all, you wouldn't want to have to say
yes to everything everyone ever wanted from you, either. In addition,
some things are not that important.

But this does not mean that you won't have feelings about not getting what you want. The "free" response—and the response that will
also leave you free—is sadness. Instead of becoming angry and trying

to control the situation, accept the fact that we don't always get what we want; that is part of life and part of love. So, be sad for a moment and say to yourself or the other person, "Rats! Bummer! That's sad. I really wanted that. Oh, well. Onward!" Or something like that. It denotes that you are taking responsibility for your own wants and not having a temper tantrum when you do not get your way. Then the relationship can go on in its normal ebb and flow.

2. If the Want Is Really Important to You, Accept the No, But Dialogue

Sometimes what you want may be really important to you and to the relationship itself. It is much bigger than a ride to the mall or how you will spend a particular vacation or where you will go on a date. It concerns your core values or signals a change of direction in your relationship. That request from the woman who wanted one weekend night of her boyfriend's time is a good example of that.

Just because your wants are your responsibility doesn't mean you should roll over and play dead when they are not granted. How boring! Persistence can be a great quality, but there are good ways and bad ways to be persistent. Sometimes the person might not even be aware of how important something is to you. Also, his or her no may come from some other reason you need to explore.

So, if you are going to take responsibility for your wants and desires, yet take a strong stand for them, how can you do that? Let's look at some ways:

Communicate the Importance of Your Request

Here are some illustrations of how you can communicate to the other person how important your request is to you:

"I understand that you don't want to give up a day with your buddies. I know you enjoy that, and I want you to have time with friends. But maybe you don't know how important the weekend time together is for me. Let me describe it to you.

During the week we are both so busy I really miss you. Then, if we miss each other on the weekends as well, I go into the next week feeling really disconnected. I want more from our relationship than that. To you, it may just seem like an afternoon. To me, it sets a pattern for an entire week. Do you understand that?"

"When I asked you to swap schedules with me, did you understand what was behind that? If it seemed like something small to me, I might have not made myself clear. It really is important. I don't want to put pressure on you, but at the same time, if you are going to say no, I want you to know what you are saying no to."

Even an "Are you sure? Please . . . I really want to do this" can communicate how strongly you feel about your request. Timidity never got anyone anything. We are not opposed to strong requests and good assertiveness. Even God says he responds to that when he sees how much someone really wants something he has previously said no to. (For example, see Genesis 18:20–32.) Make your case known. Persist. Present a good argument. This is important in every relationship, from the hostess at the restaurant who says they have no openings to a spouse or a business relationship. Every good salesman knows how to deal with objections and to be bold. Listen to what Jesus says about asking:

> "Suppose one of you has a friend, and he goes to him at midnight and says, 'Friend, lend me three loaves of bread, because a friend of mine on a journey has come to me, and I have nothing to set before him.'
>
> "Then the one inside answers, 'Don't bother me. The door is already locked, and my children are with me in bed. I can't get up and give you anything.' I tell you, though he will not get up and give him the bread because he is his friend, yet because of the man's boldness he will get up and give him as much as he needs.
>
> "So I say to you: Ask and it will be given to you; seek and you will find; knock and the door will be opened to you. For every-

one who asks receives; he who seeks finds; and to him who knocks, the door will be opened" (Luke 11:5–10).

Many times the other person, who has already said no, will "get" it: "Oh, I understand now. I didn't know it was such a big deal to you. I can see why this is so important."

It is true with God, and it is true with each other as well. Sometimes we just have to make the case for what we want and be persistent. Again, attitude is important. Don't persecute, judge, or react. Don't make the other person feel bad, and let him know he is still free to say no. Then, if you get the picture that the no is firm, deal with your sadness and move on. Even in moving on, you might also say that you would like to revisit the issue at a later date.

Seek to Understand the Reason for No

Sometimes someone says no, not because of the request, but because he or she is resisting something else in the request. If what you want is very important to you, try to find out the reason for the no. Inquire further without being controlling:

Sarah: "Help me understand why you don't want to go to the ballet."

Bob: "I had planned to go to the library that night and do some research about my fishing trip in the spring. It's the only night I can do that."

Sarah: "So you are not against going to the ballet with me. You want to go to the library and do research."

Bob: "Right."

Sarah: "Okay, so why isn't there another night you can go to the library?"

Bob: "Because I have to go to class on Tuesday, and the other nights you have your meetings."

Sarah: "Well, what if I skipped my meeting on Monday, and we went that night instead? Would you be willing to do that?"

Bob has a reason that he can't go to the ballet. When the reason is explored, new possibilities open up. This seems simple, but it is amazing how couples and friends often do not get to a workable solution because of either control issues, reactivity, or the inability of the one who wants something to take responsibility for finding a workable solution.

Empathize and Re-ask

At times, a person's no is reflexive or not very well thought through. Sometimes it is a reaction to longstanding control issues, and he or she simply says no to assert his or her autonomy, much like a toddler. Without being controlling, angry, or demanding, just empathize and re-ask:

"It sounds like it seems like a lot to you, huh? I understand that. Still, I really want to do this."

"I realize this would mean some effort on your part. I know that. But I really want it. It is important to me. I wouldn't persist if it weren't."

"I can see that this is going to be hard on you. Still, I think it's an important thing."

Connecting and empathizing with the initial difficulty someone feels is often enough to build a bridge of understanding. It allows him or her to see how important it is to you.

Closely akin to this is listening to a person's objections. When the other person objects, inquire more. Listen. Ask for more information:

Tom: "I can't do that. It would cause me so much trouble with my schedule. No way."

Ellie: "Really? That sounds hard. Tell me more. I want to get it."

Tom: "Well, it means that I would have to go to the boss and change things around."

Ellie: "Yeah, I understand. That would be uncomfortable, especially with the way he can be. What do you think he would say?"

Tom: "There's no telling. He might blow up. How can I know?"

Ellie: "Brutal! What do you do when he does that? That sounds like a lot of pressure."

Tom: "You're darn right it is. I hate it!"

Ellie: "Okay, I can see that this is no small thing. And it's going to be a sacrifice. I understand that even better than I did. But I still want you to go forward for me in this."

Remember, this is not a tug of war. It is two people trying to come together and know that they are understood. Even if the person says yes, you would want to fully understand what is being given so you can be properly grateful. Thus, inquire if you need to.

Deal with Defensiveness

Sometimes the person may get defensive with you in his reflexive no or invite you to an argument. If this happens, just remain centered on what you want. Empathize, then go back to your desire. State it plainly and clearly, and do not try to justify it or answer the person's defensiveness:

Tom: "What? You are always wanting something from me. I can't believe you want me to go to that. Can't you see I'm busy? Do you think I don't have anything to do myself?"

Ellie: "I understand you have a lot to do. But I want to do this."

Tom: "See, there you go! Just thinking about yourself again. What about me?"

Ellie: "I know it seems like that to you. Sorry! But this is something that I really want."

Tom is sending Ellie a lot of invitations to get off track. But Ellie does a good job of empathizing with his defensiveness and not getting sucked in. If she had, she would indeed have gotten off track and gone down the wrong road. Consider this response:

Ellie: "That's not true! I don't always want something, and I try all the time to help you when you are busy. Just the other day. . . ."

Or another response:

> **Ellie:** "When do I think about myself? Just give me an example. I think I am very giving around here. What do you mean by that?"

Instead of giving either response, Ellie just stayed clear, kept in touch with what she wanted, and stated it. The person is free to say no, but not free to get you off track or into an argument.

Emphasize Real Consequences

Tom and Sandy were in a demanding season of life with his work and rearing three small children. He was an attorney who had taken on a tough case that required many nights at the office and much weekend travel for the better part of a year. Although it was one of those "have to do it" seasons of work many professions require, the strain on him was showing. When he had decided to go to law school, Sandy and Tom both understood the future demands of the job, but together they committed to it. They were willing to make sacrifices because they both enjoyed the fruits of his work.

But when Tom worked, Sandy was stuck with three young children all of the time they were awake. She had little time either to herself or with Tom. She was weathering it well, however, because she knew he was suffering too.

The problem arose when Tom got some unexpected time off. Every now and then someone would cancel, and he would not have to work that day. When this happened, Tom would go fishing to "get away from it all." Sandy did not mind his fishing, and she even wanted him to have relaxation time. But while he was getting his time, she was getting none.

Several times, when he got time off, she had asked him if they could do something as a family or if he could keep the kids so she could do something for herself. Each time, he said, "No, I have to go fishing and get away."

After this had happened a few times, Sandy decided to do something about it. Until then, she had communicated in noncontrolling ways.

She had understood his need for time to himself, and she had provided ways for him to have that. At the same time, she had persisted in making her case for why it was also important for her to have time to herself and time with him. Still, Tom took only himself into consideration. So she accepted his no, but she let him know that his actions were having real consequences:

Sandy: "Tom, I understand you have a lot of work, and I know you don't get much time off and need some time to get away. But I think I have been pretty gracious about giving that time to you. Whenever you've had a day off, you've taken it for yourself. I've been happy for you, but I would like some time for me and for us. Each time I have asked for that, you have gone fishing anyway.

"I don't want to punish you for that, but I want to let you know the effect it's having on me. I used to ask you for time because I wanted to spend it with you. I desired it. I felt a warm longing for you. But since you have been denying me time, my feelings are changing. I have started to feel more distant from you. I'm feeling far away from you and not like we are partners in this together. I'm not trying to get on your case, but I am trying to let you know the truth of what's happening inside me as you continue to choose to use all of your free time for yourself. I'm not here to argue about this. It's just true. And I want you to know that it's a serious issue."

Tom: "But you have no idea how hard I'm working. I'm doing this for us, and it's killing me. You don't understand how hard it is on me."

Sandy: "I understand how you feel. I feel for you as well. What I am telling you is what is happening inside me. I can't be close to you on an 'on call' basis unless I'm feeling that you are showing some desire to move toward me too. I don't want you to respond right now. I have already talked about it enough to let you know how it is affecting me. I would like you to think about it. I want you to commit to our getting some counseling together. If you won't either change things or go talk to someone with me, I'm going to have to do something for myself. I'm not doing well the way things are. If you won't join me, I'll have to begin to take care of me by myself."

Tom: "What does that mean? What are you going to do, leave?"

Sandy: "I don't know what I am going to do. I'm not going to talk about that right now. What I am telling you is that this is getting serious, and I want you to either change or go to counseling with me. If you won't do either, I will deal with that when it happens. I'm just telling you the way it is with me. I love you and want this to change."

Notice that Sandy didn't get hooked into Tom's defensiveness or his invitation to get off track. She persisted in letting him know that, although he was free to continue to say no to her requests, he would experience consequences if he did.

If one spouse's relationship "wants" are not fulfilled, the other spouse will reap a loss of intimacy and closeness in the marriage. If a husband like Tom never gives time up from his hobbies or work to be with his wife, he risks losing intimacy with her. These are real consequences.

Find a Balance

Every good relationship has a balance of yeses and nos. If you never said no to anything, you would be a puppet. If you never said yes, you would be a dictator. In the middle is the give and take of a good relationship, in which you negotiate and persist when something is important to you.

When trying to find a balance, remember that there is a difference between wants and needs. Both are valid. Both are important. (In a paradoxical way, we "need" both.) There are some things we need, things we can't live without. Things we need are different from things we want—things that would make life better or more enjoyable. We naturally have to take a stronger stand on asserting needs and getting them met.

What's the difference between a need and a want? Recall how we defined this earlier: When a need is not met, we suffer injury. Here are some needs worth standing up for:

- Our need for connection
- Our need for freedom from control
- Our need for unconditional love
- Our need for equality and mutuality
- Our need for physical safety
- Our need for emotional and mental safety
- Our need to express talents and interests
- Our need for rest
- Our need for pleasure
- Our need for healing

These needs are worth fighting for more than wants that only make life or a relationship better or more fulfilling. Relationships are, at times, going to fail to make us happy and fulfilled. At those times, people commit to doing without while they solve those problems. So don't act as if everything you want is a need and that your relationship should be providing your every want. Reserve that stance for serious infractions.

But remember, even serious infractions by your partner are still your responsibility. If, for example, you are in a marriage where there is no connection or in which your spouse has an addiction that is making things emotionally unsafe, it is still your responsibility to deal with things appropriately. Go get support for your need for emotional stability, safety, and healing. Don't be a victim.

When you go outside the relationship to have those needs met, have them met in *a way that will support the healing of the relationship*. If your spouse has an addiction, for example, and that is why your needs are not being met, get support and connection from a co-dependency or co-addicts support group or counselor, not a relationship that could potentially lead to an affair. Choose the *redemptive* way of getting your needs met: "Do not be overcome by evil, but overcome evil with good" (Rom. 12:21).

In the arena of preferences, be "sad" when you don't get what you want instead of making someone "bad." Don't make yourself bad for wanting things, and don't make the other person bad for not granting them. Be proactive about getting your needs and wishes met inside the relationship, and if that does not happen, get them met somewhere else. But again, don't do it in a way that is destructive to the relationship. Keep yourself free from bitterness, and keep the other person free from control. In the long run you will get more love and satisfaction, and you will get what you want.

NEW INTERNATIONAL VERSION

STUDENT BIBLE

Student Bible, Large Print

The best-selling *Student Bible*—for adult readers who want to better understand the Bible

If you think the *Student Bible* is just for students, guess again. What this best-selling, award-winning study Bible has done for <u>over 5 million</u> readers on the high school and college levels, it also accomplishes for men and women who are raising families, holding down careers, and dealing with the challenges and responsibilities of life. If you consider yourself a lifelong student of God's Word—if you turn to the Bible for wisdom and guidance in an uncertain world—then you'll value the *Student Bible's* proven, commonsense approach to studying the Scriptures.

The *Student Bible, Large Print* is perfect for adult readers who desire a thoughtful approach to studying and understanding the Bible. Edited by award-winning authors **Philip Yancey** and **Tim Stafford,** this Bible will enable you to understand what you read, find the topics you're looking for, and make real progress in your studies. You'll appreciate this Bible's journalistic style and well-conceived features. Using material from Philip Yancey and Brenda Quinn's book *Meet the Bible,* the *Student Bible* takes you on a fascinating and enriching six-month tour of the entire Bible—its characters, places, times, stories, and meaning. New discoveries await you every day. And this large-print edition makes reading easy.

Features Include:

- **Guided Tour of the Bible** takes you on a 180-day journey featuring daily points of interest
- **3-Track Reading Plan** lets you read at your own pace
- **Highlights and Insights** explain difficult verses, point out important facts and encourage reflection
- **Large, 11-point type** is easy to read
- **Red-letter words of Christ**
- **Book Introductions and Overviews** summarize the content and point out important themes and characters for each book of the Bible
- **Updated Subject Guide** points to the Bible's message on topics of interest
- **100 People You Should Know** gives insight into the lives and faith of important biblical people
- **Updated Glossary of Non-Biblical People and Places**

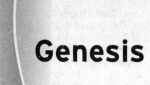

Genesis

INTRODUCTION

God at Work
Everything—literally everything—begins here

2:3 *And God blessed the seventh day and made it holy, because on it he rested from all the work of creating that he had done.*

The Bible begins with words that have become famous: "In the beginning God created." God, like an artist, fashioned a universe. How can we grasp the grandeur of this?

Michelangelo, perhaps the greatest artist in history, may help us to understand. He painted Rome's famous Sistine Chapel to retell Genesis' story of creation. His experience proves one thing: Creativity is work.

An Exhausting Effort

Michelangelo had 6,000 square feet of ceiling to cover—the size of four average house roofs. Anyone who has painted a ceiling with a paint roller has caught a hint of the physical difficulty of such a task. But Michelangelo's plan called for 300 separate, detailed portraits of men and women. For more than three years the 5'4" artist devoted all his labors to the exhausting strain of painting the vast overhead space with his tiny brushes.

Sometimes he painted standing on a huge scaffold, a paintbrush high over his head. Sometimes he sat, his nose inches from the ceiling. Sometimes he painted while lying on his back. His back, shoulders, neck and arms cramped painfully.

In the long days of summer, he had light to paint 17 hours a day, taking food and a chamber pot with him on the 60-foot scaffold. For 30 days at a stretch he slept in his clothes, not even taking off his boots. Paint dribbled into his eyes so he could barely see. Freezing in the winter, sweating in the summer, he painted until at last the ceiling looked like a ceiling no more. He had transformed it into the creation drama, with creatures so real they seemed to breathe. Never before or since have paint and plaster been so changed.

The Miracle of Life

But, as Michelangelo knew very well, his work was a poor, dim image of what God had created. Over the plaster vault of the Sistine Chapel rose the immense dome of God's sky, breathtaking in its simple beauty. Mountains, seas, the continents—all these, and much more, are the creative work of God, the Master Artist.

God's world, so much bigger and more beautiful than Michelangelo's masterpiece, is the product of incomparably greater energy. As author Eugene Peterson has written, "The Bible begins with the announcement, 'In the beginning God created,' not 'sat majestic in the heavens' and not 'was filled with beauty and love.' He created. He did something." In the beginning, God went to work.

Genesis focuses attention on this creative, hardworking God. The word *God* appears 30 times in the 31 verses of chapter 1. He grabs our attention in action. Genesis is an account of his deeds, ringing splendidly with the magnificent effort of creation.

Mending Broken Pieces

Genesis also talks about the work of humankind—but the tone changes abruptly. God had barely finished creating the universe when human rebellion marred it, like a delinquent spraying graffiti on the Sistine Chapel. Chapters 3-11 of Genesis portray a series of disasters: Adam and Eve's rebellion, Cain's calculated murder of his brother, the worldwide wickedness leading to the great flood, and human arrogance at Babel.

God immediately began to mend the pieces his creatures had broken. He narrowed his scope from the whole universe to a single man—not a king or wealthy landowner, but a childless nomad, Abraham. Abraham, Sarah, Isaac, Rebekah, Jacob, Rachel, Joseph—the upward thrust from chapter 12 on came through God's work in these startlingly human individuals. They were far from perfect, yet God picked them up where they were and carried them forward. He promised them great things. He moved through them to restore his art. His creative activity did not stop on the seventh day.

Genesis and Revelation

Many people read the Old Testament as though it portrayed the "bad old days" before Jesus. But that's not an accurate picture. Actually, the first three chapters of Genesis link to the last book of the Bible, Revelation. They are like brackets of perfection around the sadness of life marred by sin, death, suffering and hatred. In Genesis we learn that life didn't start out that way. In Revelation we find out it won't end that way either. But the Old and New Testaments take place between those brackets. Through Abraham, through Moses, ultimately in Jesus, God is hard at work to make things right.

How to Read **Genesis**

Genesis is one of the most enjoyable Old Testament books, full of memorable stories of people and events. It is a crucial book to know, for the rest of the Bible often refers back to it.

Genesis tells the story of many beginnings—the beginning of the universe; the beginning of sin; and perhaps most important, the beginning of God's work to restore a sinful humanity.

The book breaks into two major sections. The first 11 chapters take a big view. They give the origins of human society, including the familiar stories of Adam and Eve, Cain and Abel, Noah's ark and the tower of Babel. Here, a few words carry great significance. You need to read slowly and reflectively, for what happens in a single line may echo off events for centuries to come. For instance, Adam and Eve's sin, because it was the first sin, became an emblem of disobedience against God.

Beginning at chapter 12, Genesis tells a different kind of story—that of a single family. The pace of the story slows to develop the personalities of Abraham, Isaac, Jacob and Joseph. These fathers and sons are full of human faults and oddities. Do you recognize any of their traits in people you know?

Seeing their fully human personalities, try to understand what God's plans were for them as individuals—and through them, for the restoration of a whole world marred by sin.

High Points in Genesis

The following chapters from Genesis are of special note, and included in the Guided Tour of the Bible reading plan. See page xii for further details.

Chapter 1: the story of creation.
Chapter 2: Adam and Eve.
Chapter 3: sin enters a perfect world.
Chapter 4: Cain and Abel.
Chapter 7: Noah and the great flood.

Chapter 8: the end of the great flood.
Chapter 15: God's covenant with Abraham.
Chapter 19: the destruction of Sodom and Gomorrah.
Chapter 22: God's testing of Abraham.
Chapter 27: Jacob cheats his brother Esau.
Chapter 28: Jacob, fleeing Esau, dreams about God.
Chapter 37: Joseph is sold into slavery.
Chapter 41: Joseph rises to the highest position in Egypt.
Chapter 45: Joseph reveals his identity to his brothers.

People You'll Meet in Genesis

The Beginning

1 In the beginning God created the heavens and the earth. ²Now the earth was*a* formless and empty, darkness was over the surface of the deep, and the Spirit of God was hovering over the waters.

³ And God said, "Let there be light," and there was light. ⁴God saw that the light was good, and he separated the light from the darkness. ⁵God called the light "day," and the darkness he called "night." And there was evening, and there was morning—the first day.

⁶ And God said, "Let there be an expanse between the waters to separate water from water." ⁷So God made the expanse and separated the water under the expanse from the water above it. And it was so. ⁸God called the expanse "sky." And there was evening, and there was morning—the second day.

⁹ And God said, "Let the water under the sky be gathered to one place, and let dry ground appear." And it was so. ¹⁰God called the dry ground "land," and the gathered waters he called "seas." And God saw that it was good.

¹¹Then God said, "Let the land produce vegetation: seed-bearing plants and trees on the land that bear fruit with seed in it, according to their various kinds." And it was so. ¹²The land produced vegetation: plants bearing seed according to their kinds and trees bearing fruit with seed in it according to their kinds. And God saw that it was good. ¹³And there was evening, and there was morning—the third day.

¹⁴ And God said, "Let there be lights in the expanse of the sky to separate the day from the night, and let them serve as signs to mark seasons and days and years, ¹⁵and let them be lights in the expanse of the sky to give light on the earth." And it was so. ¹⁶God made two great lights—the greater light to govern the day and the lesser light to govern the night. He also made the stars. ¹⁷God set them in the expanse of the sky to give light on the earth, ¹⁸to govern the day and the night, and to separate light from darkness. And God saw that it was good. ¹⁹And there was evening, and there was morning—the fourth day.

a2 Or possibly became

²⁰And God said, "Let the water teem with living creatures, and let birds fly above the earth across the expanse of the sky." ²¹So God created the great creatures of the sea and every living and moving thing with which the water teems, according to their kinds, and every winged bird

---

GUIDED TOUR

Genesis 1

A Book of Beginnings:

Genesis gives the who, not the how

1:1,31 *In the beginning God created the heavens and the earth . . . God saw all that he had made, and it was very good.*

The story of the Bible—more, the history of the universe—starts with the simple declaration, "God created." The rest of this chapter fills in what he created: stars, oceans, plants, birds, fish, mammals and, finally, man and woman.

Genesis 1 says little about the processes God used in creation. You'll find no explanations of DNA or the scientific principles behind creation. For this reason, controversy springs up in classrooms, and even in courts, between those who see God's hand in creation and those who see only the blind forces of evolution at work. The opening chapter of the Bible does, however, insist on two facts:

1. *Creation is God's work.* "And God said . . . And God said . . . And God said"—this phrase beats a cadence all the way through the chapter. Butterflies, waterfalls, bottlenose dolphins, praying mantises, kangaroos—they are all God's idea. This magnificent world is like a museum displaying God's artistic genius. All that follows in the Bible reinforces the clear message of Genesis 1: Behind all of history, there is God. Every helium atom, every spiral galaxy, every living creature exists because God wants it to. Think of Genesis 1-3 as an artist's signature on a painting; God is saying, "This is mine."

2. *Creation is good.* Like a bell, another sentence tolls softly throughout this chapter: "And God saw that it was good." In our day we hear alarming reports about nature: global warming, polluted oceans, vanishing species, the destruction of rain forests. Much has changed, much has been spoiled, since creation. Genesis 1 describes the unspoiled world God designed. Whatever beauty we sense in nature today echoes, however faintly, that pristine state.

In fact, the Bible opens and closes with much the same scenery: a garden, watered by a river, with human beings living in the actual presence of God. The two scenes are like brackets of perfection around the history of a badly scarred planet.

Captain Frank Borman, one of America's Apollo astronauts, read this very chapter on a telecast from outer space during the Christmas season. As he gazed out his window, he saw Earth as a brightly colored ball, hanging alone in the darkness of space. It looked at once awesomely beautiful and terribly fragile. It looked like the view from Genesis 1.

Life Questions

Think of a time when you noticed—really noticed—the beauty of the natural world.

To continue the "Guided Tour" reading plan, turn to p. 6. You can find the overall plan on p. xii.

according to its kind. And God saw that it was good. 22God blessed them and said, "Be fruitful and increase in number and fill the water in the seas, and let the birds increase on the earth." 23And there was evening, and there was morning—the fifth day.

24 And God said, "Let the land produce living creatures according to their kinds: livestock, creatures that move along the ground, and wild animals, each according to its kind." And it was so. 25God made the wild animals according to their kinds, the livestock according to their kinds, and all the creatures that move along the ground according to their kinds. And God saw that it was good.

26Then God said, "Let us make man in our image, in our likeness, and let them rule over the fish of the sea and the birds of the air, over the livestock, over all the earth,*a* and over all the creatures that move along the ground."

27 So God created man in his own image, in the image of God he created him; male and female he created them.

28God blessed them and said to them, "Be fruitful and increase in number; fill the earth and subdue it. Rule over the fish of the sea and the birds of the air and over every living creature that moves on the ground."

29Then God said, "I give you every seed-bearing plant on the face of the whole earth and every tree that has fruit with seed in it. They will be yours for food. 30And to all the beasts of the earth and all the birds of the air and all the creatures that move on the ground—everything that has the breath of life in it—I give every green plant for food." And it was so.

31God saw all that he had made, and it was very good. And there was evening, and there was morning—the sixth day.

2 Thus the heavens and the earth were completed in all their vast array.

2 By the seventh day God had finished the work he had been doing; so on the seventh day he rested*b* from all his work. 3And God blessed the seventh day and made it holy, because on it he rested from all the work of creating that he had done.

Adam and Eve

4This is the account of the heavens and the earth when they were created.

When the LORD God made the earth and the heavens— 5and no shrub of the field had yet appeared on the earth*c* and no plant of the field had yet sprung up, for the LORD God had not sent rain on the earth*c* and there was no man to work the ground, 6but streams*d* came up from the earth and watered the whole surface of the ground— 7the LORD God formed the man*e* from the dust of the ground and breathed into his nostrils the breath of life, and the man became a living being.

8Now the LORD God had planted a garden in the east, in Eden; and there he put the man he had formed. 9And the LORD God made all kinds of trees grow out of the ground—trees that were pleasing to the eye and good for food. In the middle of the garden were the tree of life and the tree of the knowledge of good and evil.

10A river watering the garden flowed from Eden; from there it was separated into four headwaters. 11The name of the first is the Pishon; it winds through the entire land of Havilah, where there is gold. 12(The gold of that land is good; aromatic resin*f* and onyx are also there.) 13The name of the second river is the Gihon; it winds through the entire land of Cush.*g* 14The name of the third river is the Tigris; it runs along the east side of Asshur. And the fourth river is the Euphrates.

a26 Hebrew; Syriac *all the wild animals*   *b2* Or *ceased*; also in verse 3   *c5* Or *land*; also in verse 6   *d6* Or *mist*   *e7* The Hebrew for *man (adam)* sounds like and may be related to the Hebrew for *ground (adamah)*; it is also the name *Adam* (see Gen. 2:20).   *f12* Or *good; pearls*   *g13* Possibly southeast Mesopotamia

¹⁵The LORD God took the man and put him in the Garden of Eden to work it and take care of it. ¹⁶And the LORD God commanded the man, "You are free to eat from any tree in the garden; ¹⁷but you must not eat from the tree of the knowledge of good and evil, for when you eat of it you will surely die."

¹⁸The LORD God said, "It is not good for the man to be alone. I will make a helper suitable for him."

¹⁹Now the LORD God had formed out of the ground all the beasts of the field and all the birds of the air. He brought them to the man to see what he would name them; and whatever the man called each living creature, that was its name. ²⁰So the man gave names to all the livestock,

---

GUIDED TOUR

Genesis 2

Continued from page 4

One Shining Moment: *The world as God intended it*

2:7 *The LORD God formed the man from the dust of the ground and breathed into his nostrils the breath of life, and the man became a living being.*

After presenting the cosmic view in chapter 1, Genesis repeats the story of creation, this time narrowing the focus to human beings. We alone, of all God's works, are made in God's image (1:26). People disagree on what exactly the phrase "image of God" means. Does it refer to immortality? Intelligence? Creativity? Relationship? Perhaps we understand its meaning best by thinking of "the image of God" as a kind of mirror. God created human beings so that by looking upon them he sees reflected something of himself.

Genesis makes the point that human beings differ profoundly from the rest of creation. We recognize this difference instinctively: The law has a different penalty for killing an animal than it has for killing a person. Human life is "sacred." Alone of all creation, human beings receive the breath of life from God himself.

History Set in Motion

Genesis 2 shows human history just getting under way. Marriage begins here: Even in a state of perfection, Adam feels loneliness and desire, so God provides woman. From this time on, marriage takes priority over other relationships. Work begins here too: Adam assumes a role of authority over the animals and plants. Humans begin to exercise a kind of mastery over the rest of creation.

Only the slightest hint of foreboding clouds this blissful scene of Paradise. It appears in verse 17, in the form of a single negative command from God. Adam and Eve enjoy perfect freedom with this one small exception, a test of their obedience.

Throughout history, artists have tried to re-create in words and images what a perfect world would look like: a world of love and beauty, a world with no guilt or suffering or shame. Genesis 1–2 describes such a world. For the last time in many thousands of years it could be said, "They felt no shame."

Life Questions

Think about a close friend or family member. In what way does this person reflect God? Does he or she possess a quality or personality trait that reflects what God must be like?

To continue the "Guided Tour" reading plan, turn to p. 8. You can find the overall plan on p. xii.

the birds of the air and all the beasts of the field.

But for Adam[a] no suitable helper was found. [21]So the LORD God caused the man to fall into a deep sleep; and while he was sleeping, he took one of the man's ribs[b] and closed up the place with flesh. [22]Then the LORD God made a woman from the rib[c] he had taken out of the man, and he brought her to the man.

[23]The man said,

"This is now bone of my bones
    and flesh of my flesh;
she shall be called 'woman,'[d]
    for she was taken out of man."

[24]For this reason a man will leave his father and mother and be united to his wife, and they will become one flesh.

[25]The man and his wife were both naked, and they felt no shame.

The Fall of Man

3 Now the serpent was more crafty than any of the wild animals LORD God had made. He said to the woman, "Did God really say, 'You must not eat from any tree in the garden'?"

[2]The woman said to the serpent, "We may eat fruit from the trees in the garden, [3]but God did say, 'You must not eat fruit from the tree that is in the middle of the garden, and you must not touch it, or you will die.'"

[4]"You will not surely die," the serpent said to the woman. [5]"For God knows that when you eat of it your eyes will be opened, and you will be like God, knowing good and evil."

[a]20 Or the man   [b]21 Or took part of the man's side
[c]22 Or part   [d]23 The Hebrew for woman sounds like the Hebrew for man.

---

100 people
you should know

Adam and Eve
First in Everything

They were the first human beings on Earth, part of God's original creation. As such, Adam and Eve set the standard for everything that followed. Their lives illustrate what God loves in human beings—as well as what he loathes.

First ecologists. They were the first to name animals, the first to tend a garden, the first to be placed in charge of all the creatures. They took on the huge task of caring for the earth and guiding its proper use.

First to form a relationship with God. Adam and Eve were made in God's image. God conversed with them and gave them responsibilities. When they failed God, they felt ashamed and feared meeting him.

First married couple. God himself made the introductions and gave the first couple the delight of each other, body and soul. As 2:24 suggests, this suitability is the basis for all marriages. Both Jesus and Paul quoted this passage in their comments on sex and marriage (Matthew 19:5; Mark 10:7–8; 1 Corinthians 6:16; Ephesians 5:31). Marriage led to parenthood, though the very first child (Cain) brought pain as well as joy.

First to sin against God. Although they only had to follow directions, they failed. In response to their sin, they hid from God and blamed each other. "Think of all the squabbles Adam and Eve must have had in the course of their nine hundred years," wrote Martin Luther. "Eve would say, 'You ate the apple,' and Adam would retort, 'You gave it to me.'"

In the end, the first two human beings were banished from Paradise and driven out into a world full of problems God had never intended for them to confront. In that, as in everything, these two led the way for all of us.

Life Questions

Are you in a position to set an example for others? What can you learn from Adam and Eve's experience?

⁶When the woman saw that the fruit of the tree was good for food and pleasing to the eye, and also desirable for gaining wisdom, she took some and ate it. She also gave some to her husband, who was with her, and he ate it. ⁷Then the eyes of both of them were opened, and they realized they were naked; so they sewed fig leaves together and made coverings for themselves.

⁸Then the man and his wife heard the sound of the Lord God as he was walking in the garden in the cool of the day, and they hid from the Lord God among the trees of the garden. ⁹But the Lord God called to the man, "Where are you?"

¹⁰He answered, "I heard you in the garden, and I was afraid because I was naked; so I hid."

¹¹And he said, "Who told you that you were naked? Have you eaten from the tree that I commanded you not to eat from?"

¹²The man said, "The woman you put here with me—she gave me some fruit from the tree, and I ate it."

¹³Then the Lord God said to the woman, "What is this you have done?"

The woman said, "The serpent deceived me, and I ate."

¹⁴So the Lord God said to the serpent, "Because you have done this,

"Cursed are you above all the
      livestock
   and all the wild animals!
You will crawl on your belly
   and you will eat dust
   all the days of your life.
¹⁵ And I will put enmity
   between you and the woman,

GUIDED TOUR

Continued from page 6

Genesis 3

The Crash: *Rebellion, nakedness, hiding and shame*

3:3 *But God did say, "You must not eat fruit from the tree that is in the middle of the garden, and you must not touch it, or you will die."*

"The Fall" theologians call it, but the event this chapter describes is really more like a crash. Although Adam and Eve have everything a person could want in Paradise, still a thought nags at them: *Are we somehow missing out? Is God keeping something from us?* Like all of us, they cannot resist the temptation to reach out for what lies beyond them.

Said journalist and author G.K. Chesterton, "There is only one doctrine that can be empirically verified: the doctrine of original sin." Genesis gives few details about the first sin. Many people mistakenly assume sex is involved, but something far more basic is at stake. God has labeled one tree, just one, off-limits. The real issue is, Who will set the rules—humans or God? Adam and Eve decide in favor of themselves, and the world has never been the same.

The underlying message of Genesis goes against some common assumptions about human history. According to these chapters, the world and humanity have not been gradually evolving toward a better and better state. On the contrary, long ago we wrecked against the rocks of our own pride and stubbornness.

Nobody, including God, has been satisfied with human beings since that time. Though created good, humans disobeyed God right from the beginning, and we've been suffering the consequences ever since. Genesis helps us understand why the

and between your offspring[a] and
   hers;
he will crush[b] your head,
   and you will strike his heel."

[16]To the woman he said,

"I will greatly increase your pains in
      childbearing;
   with pain you will give birth to
      children.
Your desire will be for your husband,
   and he will rule over you."

[17]To Adam he said, "Because you listened to your wife and ate from the tree
about which I commanded you, 'You
must not eat of it,'

"Cursed is the ground because of you;
   through painful toil you will eat of
      it
   all the days of your life.

[18]It will produce thorns and thistles for
      you,
   and you will eat the plants of the
      field.
[19]By the sweat of your brow
   you will eat your food
until you return to the ground,
   since from it you were taken;
for dust you are
   and to dust you will return."

[20]Adam[c] named his wife Eve,[d] because
she would become the mother of all the
living.
[21]The LORD God made garments of skin
for Adam and his wife and clothed them.
[22]And the LORD God said, "The man has
now become like one of us, knowing

[a]15 Or *seed*   [b]15 Or *strike*   [c]20 Or *The man*   [d]20 *Eve*
probably means *living.*

---

universe is so strikingly lovely, yet so terribly tragic. It is lovely because God made it. It
is tragic because he trusted it to us—and we failed.

Did God Really Say?

Adam and Eve react to their sin as anyone reacts to sin. They rationalize, try to explain
themselves and look for someone else to take the blame. The author of Genesis
pointedly notes that they also feel the need to hide. They hide from each other by
making coverings for themselves because they sense, for the first time, a feeling of
shame about being naked. Perhaps the greatest change of all occurs in their
relationship with God. Previously, they had walked and talked freely with God in the
garden, much as one would with a friend. Now, when they hear God's voice, they hide.

The three questions God asks Adam and Eve apply to anyone in hiding: (1) Where
are you? (And why are you hiding from me?) (2) Who told you
that you were naked? (And why did you believe somebody
else, not me?) (3) What is this that you have done? (And are
you ready to take responsibility for it?)

Genesis 3 tells of other profound changes that affect the
world because the creatures choose their own way rather than
their Creator's: suffering multiplies, work becomes harder, and
a new word—*death*—enters human vocabulary. Perfection is
spoiled forever. All wars, all violence, all broken relationships,
all grief and sadness trace back to this one monumental day in
the Garden of Eden.

Life Questions

*Have you ever felt
hemmed in or
stifled by one of
God's commands?
How have you
responded to this
feeling?*

To continue the "Guided Tour" reading plan, turn to p. 11. You can find the overall plan on p. xii.

good and evil. He must not be allowed to reach out his hand and take also from the tree of life and eat, and live forever." ²³So the LORD God banished him from the Garden of Eden to work the ground from which he had been taken. ²⁴After he drove the man out, he placed on the east side^a of the Garden of Eden cherubim and a flaming sword flashing back and forth to guard the way to the tree of life.

Cain and Abel

4 Adam^b lay with his wife Eve, and she became pregnant and gave birth to Cain.^c She said, "With the help of the LORD I have brought forth^d a man." ²Later she gave birth to his brother Abel.

Now Abel kept flocks, and Cain worked the soil. ³In the course of time Cain brought some of the fruits of the soil as an offering to the LORD. ⁴But Abel brought fat portions from some of the firstborn of his flock. The LORD looked with favor on Abel and his offering, ⁵but on Cain and his offering he did not look with favor. So Cain was very angry, and his face was downcast.

⁶Then the LORD said to Cain, "Why are you angry? Why is your face downcast? ⁷If you do what is right, will you not be accepted? But if you do not do what is right, sin is crouching at your door; it desires to have you, but you must master it."

⁸Now Cain said to his brother Abel, "Let's go out to the field."^e And while they were in the field, Cain attacked his brother Abel and killed him.

⁹Then the LORD said to Cain, "Where is your brother Abel?"

^a24 Or *placed in front* ^b1 Or *The man* ^c1 *Cain* sounds like the Hebrew for *brought forth* or *acquired.* ^d1 Or *have acquired* ^e8 Samaritan Pentateuch, Septuagint, Vulgate and Syriac; Masoretic Text does not have *"Let's go out to the field."*

---

100 people
you should know

Cain and Abel
Blood Brothers

Cain and Abel (Genesis 4) were the first of many feuding siblings. After them came Isaac and Ishmael, Jacob and Esau, Rachel and Leah, Joseph and his brothers. It's a theme song in Genesis and in life: Blood kin have a hard time getting along, and they can make bitter rivals.

Cain offered a sacrifice to God, and then killed his brother when he learned God had honored Abel's offering. Genesis does not specify why God preferred Abel's offering to Cain's. (Later in the Old Testament, God accepted both animal and agricultural offerings.) Quite possibly, Cain's problem was his attitude (see Hebrews 11:4). Regardless, Cain lost his temper when things did not go his way.

The Bible tells us little about Abel and a good deal about Cain. Sadly, that makes sense because, as sinful humans, we see more of ourselves in Cain than in Abel. Cain wore his emotions on his sleeve: first jealous anger, then defensiveness, and finally shame and fear. In response to his great crime, God both punished and protected Cain. Banished from home and forced to wander all his life, he nevertheless received a measure of protection, "the mark of Cain" (4:15).

Cain's children set the pattern for humanity as it has lived ever since, a mixture of good and bad. On the one hand, as musicians, metalworkers and farmers, they helped civilize the earth. On the other hand, Cain's problems got passed down to future generations. Where Cain felt shame for his crime and punishment, his descendant Lamech would boast about his own murderous deed (4:23-24).

LifeQuestions:

Which of Cain's responses to God—anger, defensiveness, fear, shame—do you identify with most easily?

"I don't know," he replied. "Am I my brother's keeper?"

¹⁰The Lord said, "What have you done? Listen! Your brother's blood cries out to me from the ground. ¹¹Now you are under a curse and driven from the ground, which opened its mouth to receive your brother's blood from your hand. ¹²When you work the ground, it will no longer yield its crops for you. You will be a restless wanderer on the earth."

¹³Cain said to the Lord, "My punishment is more than I can bear. ¹⁴Today you are driving me from the land, and I will be hidden from your presence; I will be a restless wanderer on the earth, and whoever finds me will kill me."

¹⁵But the Lord said to him, "Not so*ᵃ*; if anyone kills Cain, he will suffer ven-

ᵃ15 Septuagint, Vulgate and Syriac; Hebrew Very well

GUIDED TOUR

Genesis 4

Continued from page 8

Crouching at the Door:
The world as God did not intend it

4:7 "If you do what is right, will you not be accepted? But if you do not do what is right, sin is crouching at your door; it desires to have you, but you must master it."

In three chapters Genesis has set the stage for human history, and now that history begins to play itself out. The first childbirth (imagine the shock!), the first formal worship, the first division of labor, the first extended families, the first cities and the first signs of culture all appear in chapter 4. But one "first" overshadows all others: the first death of a human being—a death by murder, one brother killing another.

Sin enters the world through the first family, and by the second generation people are already killing each other. The early part of Genesis shows God intervening often in response to problems in his new creation. Unable to ignore their horrible regression, God steps in with a custom-designed punishment for Cain. However, the slide continues, especially in a man named Lamech.

One Step Forward, One Step Back

Not all the news is bad. Civilization progresses rather quickly, with some people learning agriculture, some choosing to work with tools of bronze and iron, and some discovering music and the arts. In this way, human beings begin to fulfill their assigned role as stewards over the created world.

Despite these advances, history continues to slide along the track of rebellion. Every person who follows Adam and Eve faces the same choice: to obey or to disobey God's word. With numbing monotony, all make the same choice as their original parents made.

God's warning to Cain applies to everyone: "If you do not do what is right, sin is crouching at your door; it desires to have you, but you must master it."

Life Questions

What do you think you would say if God appeared in person to confront you about your sin?

To continue the "Guided Tour" reading plan, turn to p. 15. You can find the overall plan on p. xii.

geance seven times over." Then the LORD put a mark on Cain so that no one who found him would kill him. ¹⁶So Cain went out from the LORD's presence and lived in the land of Nod,ᵃ east of Eden.

¹⁷Cain lay with his wife, and she became pregnant and gave birth to Enoch. Cain was then building a city, and he named it after his son Enoch. ¹⁸To Enoch was born Irad, and Irad was the father of Mehujael, and Mehujael was the father of Methushael, and Methushael was the father of Lamech.

¹⁹Lamech married two women, one named Adah and the other Zillah. ²⁰Adah gave birth to Jabal; he was the father of those who live in tents and raise livestock. ²¹His brother's name was Jubal; he was the father of all who play the harp and flute. ²²Zillah also had a son, Tubal-Cain, who forged all kinds of tools out ofᵇ bronze and iron. Tubal-Cain's sister was Naamah.

²³Lamech said to his wives,

"Adah and Zillah, listen to me;
    wives of Lamech, hear my words.
I have killedᶜ a man for wounding me,
    a young man for injuring me.
²⁴If Cain is avenged seven times,
    then Lamech seventy-seven times."

²⁵Adam lay with his wife again, and she gave birth to a son and named him Seth,ᵈ saying, "God has granted me another child in place of Abel, since Cain killed him." ²⁶Seth also had a son, and he named him Enosh.

At that time men began to call onᵉ the name of the LORD.

From Adam to Noah

5 This is the written account of Adam's line.

When God created man, he made him in the likeness of God. ²He created them male and female and blessed them. And when they were created, he called them "man.ᶠ"

³When Adam had lived 130 years, he had a son in his own likeness, in his own image; and he named him Seth. ⁴After Seth was born, Adam lived 800 years and had other sons and daughters. ⁵Altogether, Adam lived 930 years, and then he died.

⁶When Seth had lived 105 years, he became the fatherᵍ of Enosh. ⁷And after he became the father of Enosh, Seth lived 807 years and had other sons and daughters. ⁸Altogether, Seth lived 912 years, and then he died.

⁹When Enosh had lived 90 years, he became the father of Kenan. ¹⁰And after he became the father of Kenan, Enosh lived 815 years and had other sons and daughters. ¹¹Altogether, Enosh lived 905 years, and then he died.

¹²When Kenan had lived 70 years, he became the father of Mahalalel. ¹³And after he became the father of Mahalalel, Kenan lived 840 years and had other sons and daughters. ¹⁴Altogether, Kenan lived 910 years, and then he died.

¹⁵When Mahalalel had lived 65 years, he became the father of Jared. ¹⁶And after he became the father of Jared, Mahalalel lived 830 years and had other sons and daughters. ¹⁷Altogether, Mahalalel lived 895 years, and then he died.

¹⁸When Jared had lived 162 years, he became the father of Enoch. ¹⁹And after he became the father of Enoch, Jared lived 800 years and had other sons and daughters. ²⁰Altogether, Jared lived 962 years, and then he died.

²¹When Enoch had lived 65 years, he became the father of Methuselah. ²²And after he became the father of Methuselah, Enoch walked with God 300 years and had other sons and daughters. ²³Altogether, Enoch lived 365 years. ²⁴Enoch walked with God; then he was no more, because God took him away.

²⁵When Methuselah had lived 187 years, he became the father of Lamech.

ᵃ16 Nod means wandering (see verses 12 and 14).
ᵇ22 Or who instructed all who work in   ᶜ23 Or I will kill
ᵈ25 Seth probably means granted.   ᵉ26 Or to proclaim
ᶠ2 Hebrew adam   ᵍ6 Father may mean ancestor; also in verses 7-26.

5:24 The Man Who Did Not Die

All but one of the brief biographies in chapter 5 end with the words "and then he died." We know very little about the exception, Enoch, except that he walked with God. Enoch did not die; he "was no more, because God took him away." Based on this evidence, Hebrews 11:5-6 commends Enoch as a man of faith, since "without faith it is impossible to please God."

²⁶And after he became the father of Lamech, Methuselah lived 782 years and had other sons and daughters. ²⁷Altogether, Methuselah lived 969 years, and then he died.

²⁸When Lamech had lived 182 years, he had a son. ²⁹He named him Noah[a] and said, "He will comfort us in the labor and painful toil of our hands caused by the ground the LORD has cursed." ³⁰After Noah was born, Lamech lived 595 years and had other sons and daughters. ³¹Altogether, Lamech lived 777 years, and then he died.

³²After Noah was 500 years old, he became the father of Shem, Ham and Japheth.

The Flood

6 When men began to increase in number on the earth and daughters were born to them, ²the sons of God saw that the daughters of men were beautiful, and they married any of them they chose. ³Then the LORD said, "My Spirit will not contend with[b] man forever, for

6:2 The Sons of God

This mysterious description may refer to the "sons of Seth," the line of God's people from Adam to Noah, or it may refer to angels, often called "sons of God" in the Old Testament. However you interpret it, the point is that evil behavior increased in the world, a fact that led to punishment by a flood.

he is mortal[c]; his days will be a hundred and twenty years."

⁴The Nephilim were on the earth in those days—and also afterward—when the sons of God went to the daughters of men and had children by them. They were the heroes of old, men of renown.

⁵The LORD saw how great man's wickedness on the earth had become, and that every inclination of the thoughts of his heart was only evil all the time. ⁶The LORD was grieved that he had made man on the earth, and his heart was filled with pain. ⁷So the LORD said, "I will wipe mankind, whom I have created, from the face of the earth—men and animals, and creatures that move along the ground, and birds of the air—for I am grieved that I have made them." ⁸But Noah found favor in the eyes of the LORD.

⁹This is the account of Noah.

Noah was a righteous man, blameless among the people of his time, and he walked with God. ¹⁰Noah had three sons: Shem, Ham and Japheth.

¹¹Now the earth was corrupt in God's sight and was full of violence. ¹²God saw how corrupt the earth had become, for all the people on earth had corrupted their ways. ¹³So God said to Noah, "I am going to put an end to all people, for the earth is filled with violence because of them. I am surely going to destroy both them and the earth. ¹⁴So make yourself an ark of cypress[d] wood; make rooms in it and coat it with pitch inside and out. ¹⁵This is how you are to build it: The ark is to be 450 feet long, 75 feet wide and 45 feet high.[e] ¹⁶Make a roof for it and finish[f] the ark to within 18 inches[g] of the top. Put a door in the side of the ark and make lower, middle and upper decks. ¹⁷I

---

[a]29 Noah sounds like the Hebrew for comfort.   [b]3 Or My spirit will not remain in   [c]3 Or corrupt   [d]14 The meaning of the Hebrew for this word is uncertain.   [e]15 Hebrew 300 cubits long, 50 cubits wide and 30 cubits high (about 140 meters long, 23 meters wide and 13.5 meters high)   [f]16 Or Make an opening for light by finishing   [g]16 Hebrew a cubit (about 0.5 meter)

am going to bring floodwaters on the earth to destroy all life under the heavens, every creature that has the breath of life in it. Everything on earth will perish. [18]But I will establish my covenant with you, and you will enter the ark—you and your sons and your wife and your sons' wives with you. [19]You are to bring into the ark two of all living creatures, male and female, to keep them alive with you. [20]Two of every kind of bird, of every kind of animal and of every kind of creature that moves along the ground will come to you to be kept alive. [21]You are to take every kind of food that is to be eaten and store it away as food for you and for them."

[22]Noah did everything just as God commanded him.

7 The LORD then said to Noah, "Go into the ark, you and your whole family, because I have found you righteous in this generation. [2]Take with you seven[a] of every kind of clean animal, a male and its mate, and two of every kind of unclean animal, a male and its mate, [3]and also seven of every kind of bird, male and female, to keep their various kinds alive throughout the earth. [4]Seven days from now I will send rain on the earth for forty days and forty nights, and I will wipe from the face of the earth every living creature I have made."

[5]And Noah did all that the LORD commanded him.

[6]Noah was six hundred years old when the floodwaters came on the earth. [7]And Noah and his sons and his wife and his sons' wives entered the ark to escape the waters of the flood. [8]Pairs of clean and unclean animals, of birds and of all creatures that move along the ground, [9]male and female, came to Noah and entered the ark, as God had commanded Noah. [10]And after the seven days the floodwaters came on the earth.

[11]In the six hundredth year of Noah's life, on the seventeenth day of the second month—on that day all the springs of the great deep burst forth, and the floodgates of the heavens were opened.

[12]And rain fell on the earth forty days and forty nights.

[13]On that very day Noah and his sons, Shem, Ham and Japheth, together with his wife and the wives of his three sons, entered the ark. [14]They had with them every wild animal according to its kind, all livestock according to their kinds, every creature that moves along the ground according to its kind and every bird according to its kind, everything with wings. [15]Pairs of all creatures that have the breath of life in them came to Noah and entered the ark. [16]The animals going in were male and female of every living thing, as God had commanded Noah. Then the LORD shut him in.

[17]For forty days the flood kept coming on the earth, and as the waters increased they lifted the ark high above the earth. [18]The waters rose and increased greatly on the earth, and the ark floated on the surface of the water. [19]They rose greatly on the earth, and all the high mountains under the entire heavens were covered. [20]The waters rose and covered the mountains to a depth of more than twenty feet.[b,c] [21]Every living thing that moved on the earth perished—birds, livestock, wild animals, all the creatures that swarm over the earth, and all mankind. [22]Everything on dry land that had the breath of life in its nostrils died. [23]Every living thing on the face of the earth was wiped out; men and animals and the creatures that move along the ground and the birds of the air were wiped from the earth. Only Noah was left, and those with him in the ark.

[24]The waters flooded the earth for a hundred and fifty days.

8 But God remembered Noah and all the wild animals and the livestock that were with him in the ark, and he sent a wind over the earth, and the waters receded. [2]Now the springs of the

---

[a]2 Or seven pairs; also in verse 3   [b]20 Hebrew fifteen cubits (about 6.9 meters)   [c]20 Or rose more than twenty feet, and the mountains were covered

deep and the floodgates of the heavens had been closed, and the rain had stopped falling from the sky. ³The water receded steadily from the earth. At the end of the hundred and fifty days the water had gone down, ⁴and on the seventeenth day of the seventh month the ark came to rest on the mountains of Ararat. ⁵The waters continued to recede until the tenth month, and on the first day of the tenth month the tops of the mountains became visible.

⁶After forty days Noah opened the window he had made in the ark ⁷and sent out a raven, and it kept flying back and forth until the water had dried up from the earth. ⁸Then he sent out a dove to see if the water had receded from the surface of the ground. ⁹But the dove could find no place to set its feet because there was water over all the surface of the earth; so it returned to Noah in the ark. He reached out his hand and took the dove and brought it back to himself in the ark. ¹⁰He

---

G U I D E D   T O U R

Genesis 7

Under Water: *A final judgment and a second chance*

Continued from page 11

7:4 *"Seven days from now I will send rain on the earth for forty days and forty nights, and I will wipe from the face of the earth every living creature I have made."*

The downward spiral of violence and rebellion continues until God finally reaches a decision. Genesis 6:6 records what is surely the most poignant sentence ever written: "The Lᴏʀᴅ was grieved that he had made man on the earth, and his heart was filled with pain." It seems clear that the grand human experiment has failed. God, who has taken such pride in his creation, is now ready to destroy it. He can no longer tolerate the violence that has spread across the world.

Legends of a great flood exist in the records of many cultures: the Middle East, Asia, South America. One Babylonian document in particular, "The Epic of Gilgamesh," has many parallels to the account recorded in this chapter. But Genesis presents the flood as an act of God against rebellious people, not merely an accident of geography or climate. The churning waters described here stand as a symbol of how far humankind has fallen. Torrents of water sweep through towns and cities, forests and deserts, destroying every living and man-made thing.

Few Survivors

Noah's ark—a huge, ungainly boat riding out the storm—stands as a different kind of symbol, a symbol of God's mercy. God has resolved to give Earth a second chance, which explains why he orders Noah to preserve representatives from every species.

The first human beings on Earth make a mess of things, so much so that their rebellion brings down all creation. Yet God's decision to spare Noah and his family injects a message of hope. These eight people will birth future generations and carry on the story of God's undying love for his people.

Life Questions

Many people feel that good and evil, right and wrong, must be defined by each individual. Do you agree?

To continue the "Guided Tour" reading plan, turn to p. 17. You can find the overall plan on p. xii.

8:11 Peace Symbol

The dove with an olive branch stands as a symbol for peace, and the origin of that symbol traces back to this account of restored peace between God and his creation. The olive leaf carried by the dove told Noah that lower elevations (where olives grow) were above water and had sprouted new life.

waited seven more days and again sent out the dove from the ark. ¹¹When the dove returned to him in the evening, there in its beak was a freshly plucked olive leaf! Then Noah knew that the water had receded from the earth. ¹²He waited seven more days and sent the dove out again, but this time it did not return to him.

¹³By the first day of the first month of Noah's six hundred and first year, the water had dried up from the earth. Noah then removed the covering from the ark and saw that the surface of the ground was dry. ¹⁴By the twenty-seventh day of the second month the earth was completely dry.

¹⁵Then God said to Noah, ¹⁶"Come out of the ark, you and your wife and your sons and their wives. ¹⁷Bring out every kind of living creature that is with you—the birds, the animals, and all the creatures that move along the ground—so they can multiply on the earth and be fruitful and increase in number upon it."

¹⁸So Noah came out, together with his sons and his wife and his sons' wives. ¹⁹All the animals and all the creatures that move along the ground and all the birds—everything that moves on the earth—came out of the ark, one kind after another.

²⁰Then Noah built an altar to the LORD and, taking some of all the clean animals and clean birds, he sacrificed burnt offerings on it. ²¹The LORD smelled the pleasing aroma and said in his heart: "Never again will I curse the ground because of man, even though[a] every inclination of his heart is evil from child-

a 21 Or man, for

---

100 people
you should know

Noah
Starting Over

The problem with the planet God made was not its geology, biology or meteorology. The problem centered, rather, in a single species: *Homo sapiens*. Sin, spreading like a disease, had taken over human thought and action. As a result God chose to blot out much of his creation and start all over again, using Noah for this new beginning.

Characteristically, Noah obeyed right away when God announced his plans. Noah "walked with God," says Genesis (6:9). He worked hard, building a gigantic, seaworthy structure and storing up food for hundreds of animals. Repeatedly the Bible says that Noah did "just as God commanded him."

Noah and his family spent more than a year confined in the ark. When they emerged at last to step out on muddy ground, their first action was to worship God. Impressed, God made a new covenant with Noah, promising never again to destroy the earth. He urged Noah and his family to be fruitful and multiply, just as he had urged Adam and Eve in the beginning.

Life Questions

If you were given an assignment like Noah's, how would you respond?

Did this new beginning work? The last we hear of Noah shows that sin had not been remedied. Noah got drunk, shamed himself in front of his sons and cursed one of his grandsons (9:20-25). Not even a flood could solve the problem of sin, for it lives on inside the best of people, even Noah.

hood. And never again will I destroy all living creatures, as I have done.

²²"As long as the earth endures,
   seedtime and harvest,
   cold and heat,
   summer and winter,
   day and night
   will never cease."

God's Covenant With Noah

9 Then God blessed Noah and his sons, saying to them, "Be fruitful and increase in number and fill the earth. ²The fear and dread of you will fall upon all the beasts of the earth and all the birds of the air, upon every creature that moves along the ground, and

---

GUIDED TOUR

Continued from page 15

Genesis 8

The Rainbow: *God makes a solemn promise*

8:21 *"Never again will I curse the ground because of man, even though every inclination of his heart is evil from childhood."*

The gloomy tone of Genesis brightens almost immediately as this chapter tells of Noah and the few survivors landing on an earth freshly scrubbed and sprouting new life. Their first hint of the earth's healing comes from a dove that returns to the ark with an olive branch.

For the first time in years, people actually seek to please God. In his first act on land, Noah prepares an offering of thanksgiving. God responds with a solemn promise, the first of several covenants in the Bible between God and the people he loves. While later covenants apply specifically to the Israelites, this one extends to every living creature.

Adjusting to Sad Realities

The terms of the covenant reveal how deeply Adam's fall has affected creation. Humans have cast a shadow across all nature, a shadow of fear and dread that will continue to spread throughout the animal kingdom. God's covenant recognizes certain sad adjustments to the original design of the world, taking for granted that human beings will continue to kill, not only the animals, but also each other.

Even so, God promises that regardless of what might happen, never again will he destroy life on such a massive scale. God vows, in effect, to find another way to deal with the rebellion and violence of humanity, "though every inclination of his heart is evil from childhood" (8:21).

An appropriate symbol—the rainbow—marks this first recorded covenant by God. Noah, like Adam before him, has a chance for a brand-new start. He can set civilization on a whole new course. Before long, though, Noah goes the way of his predecessors. In the last glimpse Genesis gives of him, he is sprawled in his tent, drunk and naked (9:20-27).

What seems like a brand-new story turns out to be a tired recapitulation of the same old story of human failure.

Life Questions

How do you react to those in your life who make mistakes and treat you wrongly?

To continue the "Guided Tour" reading plan, turn to p. 26. You can find the overall plan on p. xii.

upon all the fish of the sea; they are given into your hands. ³Everything that lives and moves will be food for you. Just as I gave you the green plants, I now give you everything.

⁴"But you must not eat meat that has its lifeblood still in it. ⁵And for your lifeblood I will surely demand an accounting. I will demand an accounting from every animal. And from each man, too, I will demand an accounting for the life of his fellow man.

9:4 Reverence for Life

In the Garden of Eden God had provided plants for humanity's food. Here, for the first time, he gave permission to add meat to their diet. Still, an animal was not to be eaten with "its lifeblood still in it." Kosher dietary requirements kept by Orthodox Jews today derive partly from this statement. Leviticus 17:10-14 gives more detail.

The intent, many commentators believe, was to remind God's people to show reverence for life, including animal life. This passage makes clear, however, that human life has a special significance. Ironically, capital punishment in the Bible derives its legitimacy from this. Murderers who destroy human life actually attack the image of God. Therefore God demands an accounting.

---

⁶"Whoever sheds the blood of man,
    by man shall his blood be shed;
for in the image of God
    has God made man.

⁷As for you, be fruitful and increase in number; multiply on the earth and increase upon it."

⁸Then God said to Noah and to his sons with him: ⁹"I now establish my covenant with you and with your descendants after you ¹⁰and with every living creature that was with you—the birds, the livestock and all the wild animals, all those that came out of the ark with you—every living creature on earth. ¹¹I establish my covenant with you: Never again will all life be cut off by the waters of a flood; never again will there be a flood to destroy the earth."

¹²And God said, "This is the sign of the covenant I am making between me and you and every living creature with you, a covenant for all generations to come: ¹³I have set my rainbow in the clouds, and it will be the sign of the covenant between me and the earth. ¹⁴Whenever I bring clouds over the earth and the rainbow appears in the clouds, ¹⁵I will remember my covenant between me and you and all living creatures of every kind. Never again will the waters become a flood to destroy all life. ¹⁶Whenever the rainbow appears in the clouds, I will see it and remember the everlasting covenant between God and all living creatures of every kind on the earth."

¹⁷So God said to Noah, "This is the sign of the covenant I have established between me and all life on the earth."

The Sons of Noah

¹⁸The sons of Noah who came out of the ark were Shem, Ham and Japheth. (Ham was the father of Canaan.) ¹⁹These were the three sons of Noah, and from them came the people who were scattered over the earth.

²⁰Noah, a man of the soil, proceeded[a] to plant a vineyard. ²¹When he drank some of its wine, he became drunk and lay uncovered inside his tent. ²²Ham, the father of Canaan, saw his father's nakedness and told his two brothers outside. ²³But Shem and Japheth took a garment and laid it across their shoulders; then they walked in backward and covered their father's nakedness. Their faces were turned the other way so that they would not see their father's nakedness.

²⁴When Noah awoke from his wine and found out what his youngest son had done to him, ²⁵he said,

"Cursed be Canaan!
    The lowest of slaves
    will he be to his brothers."

ᵃ20 Or soil, was the first

26He also said,

"Blessed be the LORD, the God of
    Shem!
  May Canaan be the slave of
    Shem.*a*
27 May God extend the territory of
    Japheth*b*;
  may Japheth live in the tents of
    Shem,
  and may Canaan be his*c* slave."

28After the flood Noah lived 350 years.
29Altogether, Noah lived 950 years, and
then he died.

The Table of Nations

10 This is the account of Shem, Ham
and Japheth, Noah's sons, who
themselves had sons after the flood.

The Japhethites

2 The sons*d* of Japheth:
  Gomer, Magog, Madai, Javan,
  Tubal, Meshech and Tiras.
3 The sons of Gomer:
  Ashkenaz, Riphath and Togar-
  mah.
4 The sons of Javan:
  Elishah, Tarshish, the Kittim and
  the Rodanim.*e* 5(From these the
  maritime peoples spread out into
  their territories by their clans
  within their nations, each with its
  own language.)

The Hamites

6 The sons of Ham:
  Cush, Mizraim,*f* Put and Canaan.
7 The sons of Cush:
  Seba, Havilah, Sabtah, Raamah
  and Sabteca.
  The sons of Raamah:
  Sheba and Dedan.

8Cush was the father*g* of Nimrod, who
grew to be a mighty warrior on the
earth. 9He was a mighty hunter before
the LORD; that is why it is said, "Like
Nimrod, a mighty hunter before the
LORD." 10The first centers of his kingdom
were Babylon, Erech, Akkad and Calneh,
in*h* Shinar.*i* 11From that land he went to
Assyria, where he built Nineveh, Rehoboth Ir,*j* Calah 12and Resen, which is between Nineveh and Calah; that is the
great city.

13 Mizraim was the father of
  the Ludites, Anamites, Lehabites,
  Naphtuhites, 14Pathrusites, Caslu-
  hites (from whom the Philistines
  came) and Caphtorites.
15 Canaan was the father of
  Sidon his firstborn,*k* and of the
  Hittites, 16Jebusites, Amorites,
  Girgashites, 17Hivites, Arkites, Si-
  nites, 18Arvadites, Zemarites and
  Hamathites.

Later the Canaanite clans scattered
19and the borders of Canaan reached
from Sidon toward Gerar as far as Gaza,
and then toward Sodom, Gomorrah, Admah and Zeboiim, as far as Lasha.

20These are the sons of Ham by their
clans and languages, in their territories
and nations.

The Semites

21Sons were also born to Shem, whose
older brother was*l* Japheth; Shem was
the ancestor of all the sons of Eber.

22 The sons of Shem:
  Elam, Asshur, Arphaxad, Lud and
  Aram.
23 The sons of Aram:
  Uz, Hul, Gether and Meshech.*m*
24 Arphaxad was the father of*n* Shelah,
  and Shelah the father of Eber.

---

*a26 Or be his slave   b27 Japheth sounds like the Hebrew
for extend.   c27 Or their   d2 Sons may mean
descendants or successors or nations; also in verses 3, 4,
6, 7, 20-23, 29 and 31.   e4 Some manuscripts of the
Masoretic Text and Samaritan Pentateuch (see also
Septuagint and 1 Chron. 1:7); most manuscripts of the
Masoretic Text Dodanim   f6 That is, Egypt; also in verse
13   g8 Father may mean ancestor or predecessor or
founder; also in verses 13, 15, 24 and 26.   h10 Or Erech
and Akkad—all of them in   i10 That is, Babylonia
j11 Or Nineveh with its city squares   k15 Or of the
Sidonians, the foremost   l21 Or Shem, the older brother
of   m23 See Septuagint and 1 Chron. 1:17; Hebrew
Mash   n24 Hebrew; Septuagint father of Cainan, and
Cainan was the father of*

25 Two sons were born to Eber:
  One was named Peleg,[a] because
  in his time the earth was divided;
  his brother was named Joktan.
26 Joktan was the father of
  Almodad, Sheleph, Hazarmaveth,
  Jerah, 27Hadoram, Uzal, Diklah,
  28Obal, Abimael, Sheba, 29Ophir,
  Havilah and Jobab. All these were
  sons of Joktan.

30The region where they lived stretched from Mesha toward Sephar, in the eastern hill country.

31These are the sons of Shem by their clans and languages, in their territories and nations.

32These are the clans of Noah's sons, according to their lines of descent, within their nations. From these the nations spread out over the earth after the flood.

The Tower of Babel

11 Now the whole world had one language and a common speech. 2As men moved eastward,[b] they found a plain in Shinar[c] and settled there.

3They said to each other, "Come, let's make bricks and bake them thoroughly." They used brick instead of stone, and tar for mortar. 4Then they said, "Come, let us build ourselves a city, with a tower that reaches to the heavens, so that we may make a name for ourselves and not be scattered over the face of the whole earth."

5But the LORD came down to see the city and the tower that the men were building. 6The LORD said, "If as one people speaking the same language they have begun to do this, then nothing they plan to do will be impossible for them. 7Come, let us go down and confuse their language so they will not understand each other."

8So the LORD scattered them from there over all the earth, and they stopped building the city. 9That is why it was called Babel[d]—because there the LORD confused the language of the whole world. From there the LORD scattered them over the face of the whole earth.

11:6 Human Ambition

People are ambitious—they want to succeed. Genesis portrays humans as so ambitious that they try to compete with, rather than serve, God. This was Adam and Eve's sin (3:5,22), and at Babel people were at it again, in a citywide effort. God frustrated their plans by confusing their language.

From Shem to Abram

10This is the account of Shem.

Two years after the flood, when Shem was 100 years old, he became the father[e] of Arphaxad. 11And after he became the father of Arphaxad, Shem lived 500 years and had other sons and daughters.

12When Arphaxad had lived 35 years, he became the father of Shelah. 13And after he became the father of Shelah, Arphaxad lived 403 years and had other sons and daughters.[f]

14When Shelah had lived 30 years, he became the father of Eber. 15And after he became the father of Eber, Shelah lived 403 years and had other sons and daughters.

16When Eber had lived 34 years, he became the father of Peleg. 17And after he became the father of Peleg, Eber lived 430 years and had other sons and daughters.

18When Peleg had lived 30 years, he became the father of Reu. 19And after he became the father of Reu, Peleg lived 209 years and had other sons and daughters.

20When Reu had lived 32 years, he became the father of Serug. 21And after he

a25 Peleg means division. b2 Or from the east; or in the east c2 That is, Babylonia d9 That is, Babylon; Babel sounds like the Hebrew for confused. e10 Father may mean ancestor; also in verses 11-25. f12,13 Hebrew; Septuagint (see also Luke 3:35, 36 and note at Gen. 10:24) 35 years, he became the father of Cainan. 13And after he became the father of Cainan, Arphaxad lived 430 years and had other sons and daughters, and then he died. When Cainan had lived 130 years, he became the father of Shelah. And after he became the father of Shelah, Cainan lived 330 years and had other sons and daughters became the father of Serug, Reu lived 207 years and had other sons and daughters.

²²When Serug had lived 30 years, he became the father of Nahor. ²³And after he became the father of Nahor, Serug lived 200 years and had other sons and daughters.

²⁴When Nahor had lived 29 years, he became the father of Terah. ²⁵And after he became the father of Terah, Nahor lived 119 years and had other sons and daughters.

²⁶After Terah had lived 70 years, he became the father of Abram, Nahor and Haran.

²⁷This is the account of Terah.

Terah became the father of Abram, Nahor and Haran. And Haran became the father of Lot. ²⁸While his father Terah was still alive, Haran died in Ur of the Chaldeans, in the land of his birth. ²⁹Abram and Nahor both married. The name of Abram's wife was Sarai, and the name of Nahor's wife was Milcah; she was the daughter of Haran, the father of both Milcah and Iscah. ³⁰Now Sarai was barren; she had no children.

³¹Terah took his son Abram, his grandson Lot son of Haran, and his daughter-in-law Sarai, the wife of his son Abram, and together they set out from Ur of the Chaldeans to go to Canaan. But when they came to Haran, they settled there. ³²Terah lived 205 years, and he died in Haran.

The Call of Abram

12 The LORD had said to Abram, "Leave your country, your people and your father's household and go to the land I will show you.

²"I will make you into a great nation
  and I will bless you;
I will make your name great,
  and you will be a blessing.
³I will bless those who bless you,
  and whoever curses you I will curse;
and all peoples on earth
  will be blessed through you."

⁴So Abram left, as the LORD had told him; and Lot went with him. Abram was seventy-five years old when he set out from Haran. ⁵He took his wife Sarai, his nephew Lot, all the possessions they had accumulated and the people they had acquired in Haran, and they set out for the land of Canaan, and they arrived there.

⁶Abram traveled through the land as far as the site of the great tree of Moreh at Shechem. At that time the Canaanites were in the land. ⁷The LORD appeared to Abram and said, "To your offspring[a] I will give this land." So he built an altar there to the LORD, who had appeared to him.

⁸From there he went on toward the hills east of Bethel and pitched his tent, with Bethel on the west and Ai on the east. There he built an altar to the LORD and called on the name of the LORD. ⁹Then Abram set out and continued toward the Negev.

Abram in Egypt

¹⁰Now there was a famine in the land, and Abram went down to Egypt to live there for a while because the famine was severe. ¹¹As he was about to enter Egypt, he said to his wife Sarai, "I know what a beautiful woman you are. ¹²When the Egyptians see you, they will say, 'This is his wife.' Then they will kill me but will let you live. ¹³Say you are my sister, so that I will be treated well for your sake and my life will be spared because of you."

---

[a] 7 Or seed

12:13 Abraham's Half-Truth

"A lie is an attempt to deceive," according to one definition, and by that standard Abraham was lying when he claimed Sarai was his sister. Yet he was telling half the truth, for she was his half sister (20:12). Abraham pulled this same trick years later and got caught again (chapter 20). On both occasions he feared for his life, a situation in which half-truths are particularly appealing.

¹⁴When Abram came to Egypt, the Egyptians saw that she was a very beautiful woman. ¹⁵And when Pharaoh's officials saw her, they praised her to Pharaoh, and she was taken into his palace. ¹⁶He treated Abram well for her sake, and Abram acquired sheep and cattle, male and female donkeys, menservants and maidservants, and camels.

¹⁷But the LORD inflicted serious diseases on Pharaoh and his household because of Abram's wife Sarai. ¹⁸So Pharaoh

Abraham
God begins to rebuild

12:2 *"I will make you into a great nation and I will bless you; I will make your name great."*

After scanning centuries, Genesis changes dramatically at chapter 12. Leaving the big picture of world history, it settles on one lonely individual—not a great king or a wealthy landowner, but a childless nomad, Abraham.

At God's call, Abraham had uprooted himself from civilization and begun wandering in the wilderness. Like pioneer settlers everywhere, Abraham had to be tough to survive. He moved his flocks from place to place, fought wild animals, negotiated with hostile locals, searched for sources of food and water. Yet this hardly made him unique; lots of tough nomads wandered the Middle East. What made this particular wanderer so important?

God's New Way of Working

100 people *you should know* — Abraham was important, first of all, simply because God chose him. Shortly after the destruction caused by the great flood, God picked Abraham as the foundation of a new humanity. On several remarkable occasions God spoke directly to him, promising to make his family great in the land he roamed. The promises were hard to believe: Abraham's wife was barren, Abraham was getting too old to have children, and he owned no land and had no prospect of any. Nonetheless, God asked Abraham to trust him.

The second reason why Abraham matters follows from the first: When God spoke to him, Abraham listened. He was far from perfect. Sometimes he strayed from the path God put him on, lying and trying to make the promises work out in his own way. Yet in the decisive moments of life, he listened to God and obeyed. He was willing to sacrifice anything for God—even his only son. God put his brand on Abraham, the mark of circumcision. His descendants were to be forever known as "God's people."

Uncensored Truth

The life of Abraham is a fascinating story, true to life, full of bad moments as well as good. He was hardly a theologian; a more comprehensive understanding of God would have to wait for Moses. But Abraham's faith is the root of Judaism and thus of Christianity. In his encounters with God we get raw, uncensored truth: not religion invented by a philosopher, but religion as it really happens when God meets a person.

No wonder the New Testament cites Abraham more than 80 times, and Paul tells Christians they are the true descendants of Abraham (Galatians 3:6–9). Abraham's life began to unfold the story of God's long-range plans. Two thousand years later, Abraham's descendant Jesus came to fulfill the promises made to Abraham.

Life Questions

God asked Abraham to leave his home and family and go to a far-off foreign country. If you were in his place, how would you have responded? Has God ever asked anything hard or risky of you?

summoned Abram. "What have you done to me?" he said. "Why didn't you tell me she was your wife? ¹⁹Why did you say, 'She is my sister,' so that I took her to be my wife? Now then, here is your wife. Take her and go!" ²⁰Then Pharaoh gave orders about Abram to his men, and they sent him on his way, with his wife and everything he had.

Abram and Lot Separate

13 So Abram went up from Egypt to the Negev, with his wife and everything he had, and Lot went with him. ²Abram had become very wealthy in livestock and in silver and gold.

³From the Negev he went from place to place until he came to Bethel, to the place between Bethel and Ai where his tent had been earlier ⁴and where he had first built an altar. There Abram called on the name of the LORD.

13:3 On the Road

The main trade route through Canaan passed north to south through Shechem, Bethel, Hebron and Beersheba. As Abraham and later on his descendants traveled, they naturally stopped in those places. These place-names crop up again and again in the story of God's work.

⁵Now Lot, who was moving about with Abram, also had flocks and herds and tents. ⁶But the land could not support them while they stayed together, for their possessions were so great that they were not able to stay together. ⁷And quarreling arose between Abram's herdsmen and the herdsmen of Lot. The Canaanites and Perizzites were also living in the land at that time.

⁸So Abram said to Lot, "Let's not have any quarreling between you and me, or between your herdsmen and mine, for we are brothers. ⁹Is not the whole land before you? Let's part company. If you go to the left, I'll go to the right; if you go to the right, I'll go to the left."

¹⁰Lot looked up and saw that the whole plain of the Jordan was well watered, like the garden of the LORD, like the land of Egypt, toward Zoar. (This was before the LORD destroyed Sodom and Gomorrah.) ¹¹So Lot chose for himself the whole plain of the Jordan and set out toward the east. The two men parted company: ¹²Abram lived in the land of Canaan, while Lot lived among the cities of the plain and pitched his tents near Sodom. ¹³Now the men of Sodom were wicked and were sinning greatly against the LORD.

¹⁴The LORD said to Abram after Lot had parted from him, "Lift up your eyes from where you are and look north and south, east and west. ¹⁵All the land that you see I will give to you and your offspring[a] forever. ¹⁶I will make your offspring like the dust of the earth, so that if anyone could count the dust, then your offspring could be counted. ¹⁷Go, walk through the length and breadth of the land, for I am giving it to you."

¹⁸So Abram moved his tents and went to live near the great trees of Mamre at Hebron, where he built an altar to the LORD.

Abram Rescues Lot

14 At this time Amraphel king of Shinar,[b] Arioch king of Ellasar, Kedorlaomer king of Elam and Tidal king of Goiim ²went to war against Bera king of Sodom, Birsha king of Gomorrah, Shinab king of Admah, Shemeber king of Zeboiim, and the king of Bela (that is, Zoar). ³All these latter kings joined forces in the Valley of Siddim (the Salt Sea[c]). ⁴For twelve years they had been subject to Kedorlaomer, but in the thirteenth year they rebelled.

⁵In the fourteenth year, Kedorlaomer and the kings allied with him went out and defeated the Rephaites in Ashteroth Karnaim, the Zuzites in Ham, the Emites in Shaveh Kiriathaim ⁶and the Horites in the hill country of Seir, as far as El Paran

---

[a]15 Or *seed*; also in verse 16   [b]1 That is, Babylonia; also in verse 9   [c]3 That is, the Dead Sea

near the desert. [7]Then they turned back and went to En Mishpat (that is, Kadesh), and they conquered the whole territory of the Amalekites, as well as the Amorites who were living in Hazazon Tamar.

[8]Then the king of Sodom, the king of Gomorrah, the king of Admah, the king of Zeboiim and the king of Bela (that is, Zoar) marched out and drew up their battle lines in the Valley of Siddim [9]against Kedorlaomer king of Elam, Tidal king of Goiim, Amraphel king of Shinar and Arioch king of Ellasar—four kings against five. [10]Now the Valley of Siddim was full of tar pits, and when the kings of Sodom and Gomorrah fled, some of the men fell into them and the rest fled to the hills. [11]The four kings seized all the goods of Sodom and Gomorrah and all their food; then they went away. [12]They also carried off Abram's nephew Lot and his possessions, since he was living in Sodom.

[13]One who had escaped came and reported this to Abram the Hebrew. Now Abram was living near the great trees of Mamre the Amorite, a brother[a] of Eshcol and Aner, all of whom were allied with Abram. [14]When Abram heard that his relative had been taken captive, he called out the 318 trained men born in his household and went in pursuit as far as Dan. [15]During the night Abram divided his men to attack them and he routed them, pursuing them as far as Hobah, north of Damascus. [16]He recovered all the goods and brought back his relative Lot and his possessions, together with the women and the other people.

[17]After Abram returned from defeating Kedorlaomer and the kings allied with him, the king of Sodom came out to meet him in the Valley of Shaveh (that is, the King's Valley).

[18]Then Melchizedek king of Salem[b]

[a]13 Or a relative; or an ally   [b]18 That is, Jerusalem

---

100 people
you should know

Lot
Different Pathways

People who grow up close together—neighbors, friends, cousins, even siblings—sometimes end up in very different places in life. Looking back, one wonders what made the difference.

Take Lot as an example. Abraham's nephew, he apparently latched on to his uncle after losing his own father. When God called Abraham to leave home and strike out for unknown territory, Lot packed up and joined Abraham on the long trip.

Abraham reciprocated with love. Even after the two men had separated to make better use of grazing lands, Abraham cared enough about his nephew to stage a daring raid to rescue Lot from kidnappers. Later, when God announced that he would destroy Lot's adopted town of Sodom, Abraham pleaded with God to save it.

Though Lot started out close to Abraham, he ultimately chose a very different pathway. Abraham remained a nomad, following God all his days. Lot preferred the cushy surroundings of the city—despite Sodom's reputation as a center of immorality. Soon Lot grew attached.

Even when God sent angels warning him to escape the coming judgment, Lot had a hard time tearing himself away (Genesis 14). He lost everything and ended up in a cave, engaged in drunken incest with his own daughters. By contrast, the more faithful Abraham became the father of God's chosen people and one of the great patriarchs of the Old Testament.

Life Questions

If someone were to offer you a comfortable, successful position in a morally questionable situation, would you accept? Why or why not?

14:18 Mystery Man

Melchizedek appeared to Abraham without warning, received tremendous honor and then disappeared. Yet hundreds of years later he earned mention in Psalm 110, and hundreds of years after that in Hebrews 7:11–17. Melchizedek remains a mysterious figure, but he does set an important precedent for the Messiah: The same man can serve as both priest and king. (Jewish priests came from one tribe, and kings from a different tribe.) Though Melchizedek did not have the proper family lineage, his spiritual power impressed Abraham, the father of Judaism.

brought out bread and wine. He was priest of God Most High, ¹⁹and he blessed Abram, saying,

"Blessed be Abram by God Most High,
Creatorᵃ of heaven and earth.
²⁰And blessed beᵇ God Most High,
who delivered your enemies into
your hand."

Then Abram gave him a tenth of everything.

²¹The king of Sodom said to Abram, "Give me the people and keep the goods for yourself."

²²But Abram said to the king of Sodom, "I have raised my hand to the LORD, God Most High, Creator of heaven and earth, and have taken an oath ²³that I will accept nothing belonging to you, not even a thread or the thong of a sandal, so that you will never be able to say, 'I made Abram rich.' ²⁴I will accept nothing but what my men have eaten and the share that belongs to the men who went with me—to Aner, Eshcol and Mamre. Let them have their share."

God's Covenant With Abram

15 After this, the word of the LORD came to Abram in a vision:

"Do not be afraid, Abram.
I am your shield,ᶜ
your very great reward.ᵈ"

²But Abram said, "O Sovereign LORD, what can you give me since I remain childless and the one who will inheritᵉ my estate is Eliezer of Damascus?" ³And Abram said, "You have given me no children; so a servant in my household will be my heir."

⁴Then the word of the LORD came to him: "This man will not be your heir, but a son coming from your own body will be your heir." ⁵He took him outside and said, "Look up at the heavens and count the stars—if indeed you can count them." Then he said to him, "So shall your offspring be."

⁶Abram believed the LORD, and he credited it to him as righteousness.

⁷He also said to him, "I am the LORD, who brought you out of Ur of the Chaldeans to give you this land to take possession of it."

⁸But Abram said, "O Sovereign LORD, how can I know that I will gain possession of it?"

⁹So the LORD said to him, "Bring me a heifer, a goat and a ram, each three years old, along with a dove and a young pigeon."

ᵃ19 Or *Possessor*; also in verse 22   ᵇ20 Or *And praise be to*   ᶜ1 Or *sovereign*   ᵈ1 Or *shield; / your reward will be very great*   ᵉ2 The meaning of the Hebrew for this phrase is uncertain.

15:5 Offspring Like the Stars

Can you imagine the leap of faith it must have required for Abraham to accept this incredible promise? What ambivalent thoughts must have tumbled over one another in this old man's mind as he contemplated the breathtaking panorama of the heavens, without the distraction of city lights. "Count the stars . . . So shall your offspring be." From my shriveled body? From Sarah's barren womb? What kind of reaction might you have experienced? Skepticism? Sarcasm? Wonder? Comfort? Would your faith have withstood the test?

¹⁰Abram brought all these to him, cut them in two and arranged the halves opposite each other; the birds, however, he did not cut in half. ¹¹Then birds of prey came down on the carcasses, but Abram drove them away.

¹²As the sun was setting, Abram fell into a deep sleep, and a thick and dreadful darkness came over him. ¹³Then the LORD said to him, "Know for certain that your descendants will be strangers in a country not their own, and they will be

---

G U I D E D T O U R

Genesis 15

Continued from page 17

The Plan: *A new approach to restoring humanity*

15:1 *After this, the word of the Lord came to Abram in a vision.*

After a survey of dismal human failures, Genesis abruptly changes its focus, zooming in on a man named Abram (later changed to Abraham). It's almost impossible to exaggerate the importance of Abraham in the Bible. To the Jews, he represents the father of a nation, but to all of us, he represents far more. After a rocky start he grows into a towering example of faith, his relationship to God so close that for many centuries God himself is known as "the God of Abraham."

In effect, God narrows his focus on the earth by selecting one group of people with whom to develop a unique relationship. Set apart from other men and women, they become God's peculiar treasures. Rather than trying to restore the whole earth at once, God begins with a pioneer settlement, a new race that will, by example, teach the rest of the world the advantages of loving and serving God. Abraham is the father of this new race.

Abraham's Secret

Genesis 15:6 gives Abraham's secret: He "believed the LORD, and [God] credited it to him as righteousness." Abraham's trust became the foundation for a covenant between his descendants and the living God.

Dozens of other passages in the Old Testament set forth the details of God's covenant, or contract, with his chosen people. (The word *testament* means "covenant.") In this chapter God seals his promises to Abraham with a fiery vision. Abraham can expect:

Life Questions

Do people still rely on covenants, or contracts, today? What purpose do they serve?

• *A new land to live in.* Trusting God, Abraham leaves his home and travels hundreds of miles toward Canaan.
• *A large and prosperous family.* This dream obsesses Abraham and, when its fulfillment seems long in coming, tests his faith severely.
• *A great nation to come from him.* This promise does not come true until many centuries after Abraham; not until the days of David and Solomon do the Hebrew people at last become a nation.
• *A blessing to the whole world.* From the beginning, God makes it clear that he has chosen the Hebrew people, not as an end, but as a means to the ultimate goal of reaching other nations.

To continue the "Guided Tour" reading plan, turn to p. 32. You can find the overall plan on p. xii.

enslaved and mistreated four hundred years. [14]But I will punish the nation they serve as slaves, and afterward they will come out with great possessions. [15]You, however, will go to your fathers in peace and be buried at a good old age. [16]In the fourth generation your descendants will come back here, for the sin of the Amorites has not yet reached its full measure."

[17]When the sun had set and darkness had fallen, a smoking firepot with a blazing torch appeared and passed between the pieces. [18]On that day the LORD made a covenant with Abram and said, "To your descendants I give this land, from the river[a] of Egypt to the great river, the Euphrates— [19]the land of the Kenites, Kenizzites, Kadmonites, [20]Hittites, Perizzites, Rephaites, [21]Amorites, Canaanites, Girgashites and Jebusites."

Hagar and Ishmael

16 Now Sarai, Abram's wife, had borne him no children. But she had an Egyptian maidservant named Hagar; [2]so she said to Abram, "The LORD has kept me from having children. Go, sleep with my maidservant; perhaps I can build a family through her."

Abram agreed to what Sarai said. [3]So after Abram had been living in Canaan ten years, Sarai his wife took her Egyptian maidservant Hagar and gave her to her husband to be his wife. [4]He slept with Hagar, and she conceived.

When she knew she was pregnant, she began to despise her mistress. [5]Then Sarai said to Abram, "You are responsible for the wrong I am suffering. I put my servant in your arms, and now that she knows she is pregnant, she despises me. May the LORD judge between you and me."

[6]"Your servant is in your hands," Abram said. "Do with her whatever you think best." Then Sarai mistreated Hagar; so she fled from her.

[7]The angel of the LORD found Hagar near a spring in the desert; it was the spring that is beside the road to Shur. [8]And he said, "Hagar, servant of Sarai, where have you come from, and where are you going?"

"I'm running away from my mistress Sarai," she answered.

[9]Then the angel of the LORD told her, "Go back to your mistress and submit to her." [10]The angel added, "I will so increase your descendants that they will be too numerous to count."

[11]The angel of the LORD also said to her:

"You are now with child
 and you will have a son.
You shall name him Ishmael,[b]
 for the LORD has heard of your
  misery.
[12] He will be a wild donkey of a man;
 his hand will be against everyone
 and everyone's hand against him,
and he will live in hostility
 toward[c] all his brothers."

[13]She gave this name to the LORD who spoke to her: "You are the God who sees me," for she said, "I have now seen[d] the One who sees me." [14]That is why the well was called Beer Lahai Roi[e]; it is still there, between Kadesh and Bered.

[15]So Hagar bore Abram a son, and Abram gave the name Ishmael to the son she had borne. [16]Abram was eighty-six years old when Hagar bore him Ishmael.

16:2 A Substitute Wife

According to custom, a man could sleep with a servant and include her children in his household. Abraham was trying to get the children he and his wife longed for and to "help God out" in fulfilling his promise of a son. Abraham's way was not God's way, however, and Abraham's attempt led to considerable jealousy and sorrow. The same practice also led to trouble for Jacob's family (chapter 30).

---

[a]18 Or Wadi   [b]11 Ishmael means God hears.   [c]12 Or live to the east / of   [d]13 Or seen the back of   [e]14 Beer Lahai Roi means well of the Living One who sees me.

The Covenant of Circumcision

17 When Abram was ninety-nine years old, the LORD appeared to him and said, "I am God Almighty[a]; walk before me and be blameless. [2]I will confirm my covenant between me and you and will greatly increase your numbers."

[3]Abram fell facedown, and God said to him, [4]"As for me, this is my covenant with you: You will be the father of many nations. [5]No longer will you be called Abram[b]; your name will be Abraham,[c] for I have made you a father of many nations. [6]I will make you very fruitful; I will make nations of you, and kings will come from you. [7]I will establish my covenant as an everlasting covenant between me and you and your descendants after you for the generations to come, to be your God and the God of your descendants after you. [8]The whole land of Canaan, where you are now an alien, I will give as an everlasting possession to you and your descendants after you; and I will be their God."

[9]Then God said to Abraham, "As for you, you must keep my covenant, you and your descendants after you for the generations to come. [10]This is my covenant with you and your descendants after you, the covenant you are to keep: Every male among you shall be circumcised. [11]You are to undergo circumcision, and it will be the sign of the covenant between me and you. [12]For the generations to come every male among you who is eight days old must be circumcised, including those born in your household or bought with money from a foreigner—those who are not your offspring. [13]Whether born in your household or bought with your money, they must be circumcised. My covenant in your flesh is to be an everlasting covenant. [14]Any uncircumcised male, who has not been circumcised in the flesh, will be cut off from his people; he has broken my covenant."

[15]God also said to Abraham, "As for

[a]1 Hebrew *El-Shaddai* [b]5 *Abram* means *exalted father.* [c]5 *Abraham* means *father of many.*

---

100 people
you should know

Ishmael
Second Best

You might call Ishmael a mistake. His birth came about when Sarah and Abraham doubted God's promise to provide them a child in their old age. The two conspired to "help God out" by using an Egyptian servant, Hagar, as a substitute wife for Abraham. Then, when God fulfilled his promise and Sarah bore a son of her own, she cruelly drove the servant and her son out into the desert. Ishmael, the innocent victim of this scheming, suffered the consequences.

Yet God also blessed Ishmael. He "heard the boy crying" when Ishmael was nearly dying of thirst in the desert (21:17). God promised that Ishmael's descendants would comprise a great nation. The Bible records that Ishmael had 12 sons and that "the Ishmaelites" were Israel's neighbors for centuries. In fact, Arabs today traditionally trace their lineage back to Ishmael.

Ishmael apparently kept in contact with his original family; he attended Abraham's funeral, and his daughter would marry Abraham's grandson Esau. Yet his place in Abraham's "covenant" with God was lost. In a similar way, Ishmael's son-in-law Esau would enjoy the earthly blessings of success, even though God's greatest blessing was reserved for his brother Jacob. In the Bible's accounting, God's "covenant blessing" always matters more than earthly success.

Life Questions

Have you ever tried to "help God out" when you thought he couldn't, or wouldn't, help you in the way you wanted? What was the result?

Sarai your wife, you are no longer to call her Sarai; her name will be Sarah. ¹⁶I will bless her and will surely give you a son by her. I will bless her so that she will be the mother of nations; kings of peoples will come from her."

¹⁷Abraham fell facedown; he laughed and said to himself, "Will a son be born to a man a hundred years old? Will Sarah bear a child at the age of ninety?" ¹⁸And Abraham said to God, "If only Ishmael might live under your blessing!"

¹⁹Then God said, "Yes, but your wife Sarah will bear you a son, and you will call him Isaac.ᵃ I will establish my covenant with him as an everlasting covenant for his descendants after him. ²⁰And as for Ishmael, I have heard you: I will surely bless him; I will make him fruitful and will greatly increase his numbers. He will be the father of twelve rulers, and I will make him into a great nation. ²¹But my covenant I will establish with Isaac, whom Sarah will bear to

17:17 Laughing at God

Abraham was a man of faith, but his faith was less than wholehearted. Here, nearing the age of 100, he laughed heartily at God's promise that he would father a son, and he demonstrated his lack of belief by suggesting that God accept Ishmael as an adequate substitute. Some time later Sarah, his wife, shared in the "joke" (18:12).

you by this time next year." ²²When he had finished speaking with Abraham, God went up from him.

²³On that very day Abraham took his son Ishmael and all those born in his household or bought with his money, every male in his household, and circumcised them, as God told him. ²⁴Abraham was ninety-nine years old when he was circumcised, ²⁵and his son Ishmael was

ᵃ19 Isaac means he laughs.

---

100 people you should know

Sarah
Who's Laughing?

She was beautiful. She had a wonderful, wealthy husband. Sarah should have been content. Instead her life revolved around the one thing she lacked—a child. Although God had promised that her husband Abraham would father a great nation, as the decades passed Sarah remained childless. The odds of giving birth gradually dwindled. More descendants than the stars in the sky? God's promise seemed laughable as Sarah celebrated her ninetieth birthday.

A resourceful woman, Sarah came up with an alternate plan. She would use her servant Hagar as a surrogate mother. Obviously Sarah felt deep inner conflict about this decision, for when Abraham got Hagar pregnant, Sarah mistreated her and sent her away. Hagar returned, but Sarah's inner conflict persisted. She would ultimately drive both mother and son into the desert.

Meanwhile, God kept repeating the amazing promise that Sarah would become the mother of a nation. Once, Abraham fell face down and laughed incredulously at the notion. Sarah cackled too. But the joke turned on them both when old Sarah finally became pregnant. After all her years of waiting, her longings were fulfilled.

"God has brought me laughter," Sarah said when her son was born (21:6). It was a wonderful pun; in obedience to God (17:19), Abraham named his son Isaac, which means "he laughs" in Hebrew.

Life Questions

When a person has deep longings that seem impossible to fulfill, what should he or she do?

thirteen; [26]Abraham and his son Ishmael were both circumcised on that same day. [27]And every male in Abraham's household, including those born in his household or bought from a foreigner, was circumcised with him.

The Three Visitors

18 The LORD appeared to Abraham near the great trees of Mamre while he was sitting at the entrance to his tent in the heat of the day. [2]Abraham looked up and saw three men standing nearby. When he saw them, he hurried from the entrance of his tent to meet them and bowed low to the ground.

[3]He said, "If I have found favor in your eyes, my lord,[a] do not pass your servant by. [4]Let a little water be brought, and then you may all wash your feet and rest under this tree. [5]Let me get you something to eat, so you can be refreshed and then go on your way—now that you have come to your servant."

"Very well," they answered, "do as you say."

[6]So Abraham hurried into the tent to Sarah. "Quick," he said, "get three seahs[b] of fine flour and knead it and bake some bread."

[7]Then he ran to the herd and selected a choice, tender calf and gave it to a servant, who hurried to prepare it. [8]He then brought some curds and milk and the calf that had been prepared, and set these before them. While they ate, he stood near them under a tree.

[9]"Where is your wife Sarah?" they asked him.

"There, in the tent," he said.

[10]Then the LORD[c] said, "I will surely return to you about this time next year, and Sarah your wife will have a son."

Now Sarah was listening at the entrance to the tent, which was behind him. [11]Abraham and Sarah were already old and well advanced in years, and Sarah was past the age of childbearing. [12]So Sarah laughed to herself as she thought, "After I am worn out and my master[d] is old, will I now have this pleasure?"

[13]Then the LORD said to Abraham, "Why did Sarah laugh and say, 'Will I really have a child, now that I am old?' [14]Is anything too hard for the LORD? I will return to you at the appointed time next year and Sarah will have a son."

[15]Sarah was afraid, so she lied and said, "I did not laugh."

But he said, "Yes, you did laugh."

Abraham Pleads for Sodom

[16]When the men got up to leave, they looked down toward Sodom, and Abraham walked along with them to see them on their way. [17]Then the LORD said, "Shall I hide from Abraham what I am about to do? [18]Abraham will surely become a great and powerful nation, and all nations on earth will be blessed through him. [19]For I have chosen him, so that he will direct his children and his household after him to keep the way of the LORD by doing what is right and just, so that the LORD will bring about for Abraham what he has promised him."

[20]Then the LORD said, "The outcry against Sodom and Gomorrah is so great and their sin so grievous [21]that I will go down and see if what they have done is as bad as the outcry that has reached me. If not, I will know."

---

[a]3 Or *O Lord*   [b]6 That is, probably about 20 quarts (about 22 liters)   [c]10 Hebrew *Then he*   [d]12 Or *husband*

18:18   The Gospel to Abraham

God predicted here (and in several other places) that all nations on Earth would be blessed through Abraham. About two thousand years later the apostle Paul, seeing in this a prediction of God reaching out through Jews to non-Jews with the message of Christianity, wrote that God had "announced the gospel in advance to Abraham" (Galatians 3:8).

RICK WARREN

THE
PURPOSE
DRIVEN®
Life

WHAT ON EARTH AM I HERE FOR?

The most basic questions everyone faces in life are *Why am I here? What is my purpose?*

Self-help books suggest that people should look within, at their own desires and dreams, but I believe the starting place must be with God and his eternal purposes for putting us on earth.

I trust that as you read these chapters of *The Purpose-Driven® Life,* you will understand God's incredible plan for your life. The book aims to give you a big picture of what life is all about and to help you begin to live the life God created you to live.

God's five purposes for each of us are clearly explained:

- We were planned for God's pleasure—experience real worship.
- We were formed for God's family—enjoy real fellowship
- We were created to become like Christ—learn real discipleship.
- We were shaped for serving God—practice real ministry.
- We were made for a mission—live out real evangelism.

Real meaning and significance come from understanding and fulfilling God's purpose for putting us on earth. I pray that you will find your purpose with the help of *The Purpose-Driven Life.*

Pastor Rick Warren

It All Starts with God

For everything, absolutely everything,
above and below, visible and invisible, . . .
everything got started in him and
finds its purpose in him.

Colossians 1:16 (Msg)

Unless you assume a God, the question
of life's purpose is meaningless.

Bertrand Russell, atheist

It's not about you.

The purpose of your life is far greater than your own personal fulfillment, your peace of mind, or even your happiness. It's far greater than your family, your career, or even your wildest dreams and ambitions. If you want to know why you were placed on this planet, you must begin with God. You were born *by* his purpose and *for* his purpose.

The search for the purpose of life has puzzled people for thousands of years. That's because we typically begin at the wrong starting point—ourselves. We ask self-centered questions like What do *I* want to be? What should *I* do with *my* life? What are *my* goals, *my* ambitions, *my* dreams for *my* future? But focusing on ourselves will never reveal our life's purpose. The

Bible says, *"It is God who directs the lives of his creatures; everyone's life is in his power."* [1]

Contrary to what many popular books, movies, and seminars tell you, you won't discover your life's meaning by looking

Focusing on ourselves will never reveal our life's purpose.

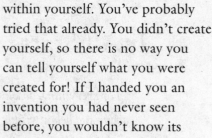

within yourself. You've probably tried that already. You didn't create yourself, so there is no way you can tell yourself what you were created for! If I handed you an invention you had never seen before, you wouldn't know its purpose, and the invention itself wouldn't be able to tell you either. Only the creator or the owner's manual could reveal its purpose.

I once got lost in the mountains. When I stopped to ask for directions to the campsite, I was told, *"You can't get there from here*. You must start from the other side of the mountain!" In the same way, you cannot arrive at your life's purpose by starting with a focus on yourself. You must begin with God, your Creator. You exist only because God wills that you exist. You were made *by* God and *for* God—and until you understand that, life will never make sense. It is only in God that we discover our origin, our identity, our meaning, our purpose, our significance, and our destiny. Every other path leads to a dead end.

Many people try to use God for their own self-actualization, but that is a reversal of nature and is doomed to failure. You were made for God, not vice versa, and life is about letting God use you for *his* purposes, not your using him for your own purpose. The Bible says, *"Obsession with self in these matters is a dead end; attention to God leads us out into the open, into a spacious, free life."* [2]

I have read many books that suggest ways to discover the purpose of my life. All of them could be classified as "self-help" books because they approach the subject from a self-centered viewpoint. Self-help books, even Christian ones, usually offer the same predictable steps to finding your life's purpose: Consider your dreams. Clarify your values. Set some goals. Figure out what you are good at. Aim high. Go for it! Be disciplined. Believe you can achieve your goals. Involve others. Never give up.

Of course, these recommendations often lead to great success. You can usually succeed in reaching a goal if you put your mind to it. But being successful and fulfilling your life's purpose are *not at all* the same issue! You could reach all your personal goals, becoming a raving success by the world's standard, and *still* miss the purposes for which God created you. You need more than self-help advice. The Bible says, *"Self-help is no help at all. Self-sacrifice is the way, my way, to finding yourself, your true self."*[3]

This is not a self-help book. It is not about finding the right career, achieving your dreams, or planning your life. It is not about how to cram more activities into an overloaded schedule. Actually, it will teach you how to do *less* in life—by focusing on what matters most. It is about becoming what *God* created you to be.

How, then, do you discover the purpose you were created for? You have only two options. Your first option is *speculation*. This is what most people choose. They conjecture, they guess, they theorize. When people say, "I've always thought life is . . . ," they mean, "This is the best guess I can come up with."

You were made by God and for God—and until you understand that, life will never make sense.

For thousands of years, brilliant philosophers have discussed and speculated about the meaning of life. Philosophy is an important subject and has its uses, but when it comes to determining the purpose of life, even the wisest philosophers are just guessing.

Dr. Hugh Moorhead, a philosophy professor at Northeastern Illinois University, once wrote to 250 of the best-known philosophers, scientists, writers, and intellectuals in the world, asking them, "What is the meaning of life?" He then published their responses in a book. Some offered their best guesses, some admitted that they just made up a purpose for life, and others were honest enough to say they were clueless. In fact, a number of famous intellectuals asked Professor Moorhead to write back and tell them if he discovered the purpose of life![4]

Fortunately, there is an alternative to speculation about the meaning and purpose of life. It's *revelation*. We can turn to what God has revealed about life in his Word. The easiest way to discover the purpose of an invention is to ask the creator of it. The same is true for discovering your life's purpose: Ask God.

God has not left us in the dark to wonder and guess. He has clearly revealed his five purposes for our lives through the Bible. It is our Owner's Manual, explaining why we are alive, how life works, what to avoid, and what to expect in the future. It explains what no self-help or philosophy book could know. The Bible says, *"God's wisdom . . . goes deep into the interior of his purposes. . . . It's not the latest message, but more like the oldest—what God determined as the way to bring out his best in us."*[5]

**DAY ONE:
IT ALL
STARTS
WITH
GOD**

God is not just the starting point of your life; he is the *source* of it. To discover your purpose in life you must turn to God's Word, not the world's wisdom. You must build your life on eternal truths, not pop psychology, success-motivation, or inspirational stories. The Bible says, *"It's in Christ that we find out who we are and what we are living for. Long before we first heard of Christ and got our hopes up, he had his eye on us, had designs on us for glorious living, part of the overall purpose he is working out in everything and everyone."*[6] This verse gives us three insights into your purpose.

1. You discover your identity and purpose through a relationship with Jesus Christ. If you don't have such a relationship, I will later explain how to begin one.

The Purpose-Driven Life

2. God was thinking of you long before you ever thought about him. His purpose for your life predates your conception. He planned it before you existed, *without your input!* You may choose your career, your spouse, your hobbies, and many other parts of your life, but you don't get to choose your purpose.

3. The purpose of your life fits into a much larger, cosmic purpose that God has designed for eternity. That's what this book is about.

Andrei Bitov, a Russian novelist, grew up under an atheistic Communist regime. But God got his attention one dreary day. He recalls, "In my twenty-seventh year, while riding the metro in Leningrad (now St. Petersburg) I was overcome with a despair so great that life seemed to stop at once, preempting the future entirely, let alone any meaning. Suddenly, all by itself, a phrase appeared: *Without God life makes no sense.* Repeating it in astonishment, I rode the phrase up like a moving staircase, got out of the metro and walked into God's light."[7]

You may have felt in the dark about *your* purpose in life. Congratulations, you're about to walk into the light.

DAY ONE
THINKING ABOUT MY PURPOSE

Point to Ponder: It's not about me.

Verse to Remember: *"Everything got started in him and finds its purpose in him."* Colossians 1:16b (Msg)

Question to Consider: In spite of all the advertising around me, how can I remind myself that life is really about living for God, not myself?

You Are Not an Accident

I am your Creator. You were in my care
even before you were born.

Isaiah 44:2a (CEV)

God doesn't play dice.

Albert Einstein

You are not an accident.

Your birth was no mistake or mishap, and your life is no fluke of nature. Your parents may not have planned you, but God did. He was not at all surprised by your birth. In fact, he expected it.

Long before you were conceived by your parents, you were conceived in the mind of God. He thought of you first. It is not fate, nor chance, nor luck, nor coincidence that you are breathing at this very moment. You are alive because God wanted to create you! The Bible says, *"The LORD will fulfill his purpose for me."*[1]

God prescribed every single detail of your body. He deliberately chose your race, the color of your skin, your hair, and every other feature. He custom-made your body just the way he wanted it. He also determined the natural talents you would possess and the uniqueness of your personality. The Bible says, *"You know me inside and out, you know every bone in my body; You know exactly how I was made, bit by bit, how I was sculpted from nothing into something."* [2]

Because God made you for a reason, he also decided *when* you would be born and *how long* you would live. He planned the days of your life in advance, choosing the exact time of your birth and death. The Bible says, *"You saw me before I was born and scheduled each day of my life before I began to breathe. Every day was recorded in your Book!"* [3]

God also planned *where* you'd be born and where you'd live for his purpose. Your race and nationality are no accident. God left no detail to chance. He planned it all for *his* purpose. The Bible says, *"From one man he made every nation, . . . and he determined the times set for them and the exact places where they should live."* [4] Nothing in your life is arbitrary. It's all for a purpose.

Most amazing, God decided *how* you would be born. Regardless of the circumstances of your birth or who your parents are, God had a plan in creating you. It doesn't matter whether your parents were good, bad, or indifferent. God knew that those two individuals possessed *exactly* the right genetic makeup to create the custom "you" he had in mind. They had the DNA God wanted to make you.

While there are illegitimate parents, there are no illegitimate children. Many children are unplanned by their parents, but they are not unplanned by God. God's purpose took into account human error, and even sin.

Long before you were conceived by your parents, you were conceived in the mind of God.

God never does anything accidentally, and he never makes mistakes. He has a reason for everything he creates. Every plant and every animal was planned by God, and every person was designed with a purpose in mind.

God's motive for creating you was his love. The Bible says, *"Long before he laid down earth's foundations, he had us in mind, had settled on us as the focus of his love."*[5]

God was thinking of you even *before* he made the world. In fact, that's why he created it! God designed this planet's environment just so we could live in it. We are the focus of his love and the most valuable of all his creation. The Bible says, *"God decided to give us life through the word of truth so we might be the most important of all the things he made."*[6] This is how much God loves and values you!

God is not haphazard; he planned it all with great precision. The more physicists, biologists, and other scientists learn about the universe, the better we understand how it is uniquely suited for our existence, custom-made with the *exact* specifications that make human life possible.

Dr. Michael Denton, senior research fellow in human molecular genetics at the University of Otago in New Zealand, has concluded, "All the evidence available in the biological sciences supports the core proposition . . . that the cosmos is a specially designed whole with life and mankind as its fundamental goal and purpose, a whole in which all facets of reality have their meaning and explanation in this central fact."[7] The Bible said the same thing thousands of years earlier: *"God formed the earth. . . . He did not create it to be empty but formed it to be inhabited."*[8]

Why did God do all this? Why did he bother to go to all the trouble of creating a universe for us? Because he is a God of love. This kind of love is difficult to fathom, but it's fundamentally reliable. You were created as a special object of God's love! God made you so he could love you. This is a truth to build your life on.

The Bible tells us, *"God is love."*[9] It doesn't say God *has* love. He *is* love! Love is the essence of God's character. There is perfect love in the fellowship of the Trinity, so God didn't *need* to create you. He wasn't lonely. But he wanted to make you in order to express his love. God says, *"I have carried you since you were born; I have taken care of you from your birth. Even when you are old, I will be the same. Even when your hair has turned gray, I will take care of you. I made you and will take care of you."* [10]

If there was no God, we would all be "accidents," the result of astronomical random chance in the universe. You could stop reading this book, because life would have no purpose or meaning or significance. There would be no right or wrong, and no hope beyond your brief years here on earth.

But there *is* a God who made you for a reason, and your life has profound meaning! We discover that meaning and purpose *only* when we make God the reference point of our lives. The Message paraphrase of Romans 12:3 says, *"The only accurate way to understand ourselves is by what God is and by what he does for us."*

This poem by Russell Kelfer sums it up:

You are who you are for a reason.
You're part of an intricate plan.
You're a precious and perfect unique design,
Called God's special woman or man.

You look like you look for a reason.
Our God made no mistake.
He knit you together within the womb,
You're *just* what he wanted to make.

The parents you had were the ones he chose,
And no matter how you may feel,
They were custom-designed with God's plan in mind,
And they bear the Master's seal.

No, that trauma you faced was not easy.
And God wept that it hurt you so;
But it was allowed to shape your heart
So that into his likeness you'd grow.

You are who you are for a reason,
You've been formed by the Master's rod.
You are who you are, beloved,
Because there is a God![11]

DAY TWO
THINKING ABOUT MY PURPOSE

Point to Ponder: I am not an accident.

Verse to Remember: *"I am your Creator. You were in my care even before you were born."* Isaiah 44:2 (CEV)

Question to Consider: I know that God uniquely created me. What areas of my personality, background, and physical appearance am I struggling to accept?

The Purpose-Driven Life

What Drives Your Life?

*I observed that the basic motive for success
is the driving force of envy and jealousy!*

Ecclesiastes 4:4 (LB)

*The man without a purpose is like
a ship without a rudder — a waif,
a nothing, a no man.*

Thomas Carlyle

Everyone's life is driven by something.

Most dictionaries define the verb *drive* as "to guide, to control, or to direct." Whether you are driving a car, a nail, or a golf ball, you are guiding, controlling, and directing it at that moment. What is the driving force in your life?

Right now you may be driven by a problem, a pressure, or a deadline. You may be driven by a painful memory, a haunting fear, or an unconscious belief. There are hundreds of circumstances, values, and emotions that can drive your life. Here are five of the most common ones:

Many people are driven by guilt. They spend their entire lives running from regrets and hiding their shame. Guilt-driven people are manipulated by memories. They allow their past to control their future. They often unconsciously punish themselves by sabotaging their own success. When Cain sinned, his guilt disconnected him from God's presence, and God said, *"You will be a restless wanderer on the earth."* [1] That describes most people today—wandering through life without a purpose.

We are products of our past, but we don't have to be prisoners of it. God's purpose is not limited by your past. He turned a murderer named Moses into a leader and a coward named Gideon into a courageous hero, and he can do amazing things with the rest of your life, too. God specializes in giving people a fresh start. The Bible says, *"What happiness for those whose guilt has been forgiven! ... What relief for those who have confessed their sins and God has cleared their record."* [2]

Many people are driven by resentment and anger. They hold on to hurts and never get over them. Instead of releasing their pain through forgiveness, they rehearse it over and over in their minds. Some resentment-driven people *"clam up"* and internalize their anger, while others *"blow up"* and explode it onto others. Both responses are unhealthy and unhelpful.

Resentment always hurts you more than it does the person you resent. While your offender has probably forgotten the offense and gone on with life, you continue to stew in your pain, perpetuating the past.

Listen: Those who have hurt you in the past cannot continue to hurt you now *unless* you hold on to the pain through resentment. Your past is past! Nothing will change it. You are only hurting yourself with your bitterness. For your own sake, learn from it, and then let it go. The Bible says, *"To worry yourself to death with resentment would be a foolish, senseless thing to do."* [3]

Many people are driven by fear. Their fears may be a result of a traumatic experience, unrealistic expectations, growing up in a high-control home, or even genetic predisposition. Regardless of the cause, fear-driven people often miss great opportunities because they're afraid to venture out. Instead they play it safe, avoiding risks and trying to maintain the status quo.

The Purpose-Driven Life

Fear is a self-imposed prison that will keep you from becoming what God intends for you to be. You *must* move against it with the weapons of faith and love. The Bible says, *"Well-formed love banishes fear. Since fear is crippling, a fearful life—fear of death, fear of judgment—is one not yet fully formed in love."*[4]

Many people are driven by materialism. Their desire to acquire becomes the whole goal of their lives. This drive to always want more is based on the misconceptions that having more will make me more happy, more important, and more secure, but all three ideas are untrue. Possessions only provide *temporary* happiness. Because things do not change, we eventually become bored with them and then want newer, bigger, better versions.

It's also a myth that if I get more, I will be more important. Self-worth and net worth are not the same. Your value is not determined by your valuables, and God says the most valuable *things* in life are not things!

The most common myth about money is that having more will make me more secure. It won't. Wealth can be lost instantly through a variety of uncontrollable factors. Real security can only be found in that which can never be taken from you—your relationship with God.

Many people are driven by the need for approval. They allow the expectations of parents or spouses or children or teachers or friends to control their lives. Many adults are still trying to earn the approval of unpleasant parents. Others are driven by peer pressure, always worried by what others might think. Unfortunately, those who follow the crowd usually get lost in it.

Nothing matters more than knowing God's purposes for your life, and nothing can compensate for not knowing them.

I don't know all the keys to success, but one key to failure is to try to please everyone. Being controlled by the opinions of others is a guaranteed way to miss God's purposes for your life. Jesus said, *"No one can serve two masters."* [5]

There are other forces that can drive your life but all lead to the same dead end: unused potential, unnecessary stress, and an unfulfilled life.

This forty-day journey will show you how to live a *purpose-driven* life—a life guided, controlled, and directed by God's purposes. Nothing matters more than knowing God's purposes for your life, and nothing can compensate for not knowing them—not success, wealth, fame, or pleasure. Without a purpose, life is motion without meaning, activity without direction, and events without reason. Without a purpose, life is trivial, petty, and pointless.

THE BENEFITS OF PURPOSE-DRIVEN LIVING

There are five great benefits of living a purpose-driven life:

Knowing your purpose gives meaning to your life. We were made to have meaning. This is why people try dubious methods, like astrology or psychics, to discover it. When life has meaning, you can bear almost anything; without it, nothing is bearable.

A young man in his twenties wrote, "I feel like a failure because I'm struggling to become something, and I don't even know what it is. All I know how to do is to get by. Someday, if I discover my purpose, I'll feel I'm beginning to live."

**DAY THREE:
WHAT
DRIVES
YOUR
LIFE?**

Without God, life has no purpose, and without purpose, life has no meaning. Without meaning, life has no significance or hope. In the Bible, many different people expressed this hopelessness. Isaiah complained, *"I have labored to no purpose; I have spent my strength in vain and for nothing."* [6] Job said, *"My life drags by—day after hopeless day"* [7] and *"I give up; I am tired of living. Leave me alone. My life makes no sense."* [8] The greatest tragedy is not death, but life without purpose.

Hope is as essential to your life as air and water. You need hope to cope. Dr. Bernie Siegel found he could predict which of his cancer patients would go into remission by asking, "Do you want to live to be one hundred?" Those with a deep sense of life purpose answered yes and were the ones most likely to survive. Hope comes from having a purpose.

If you have felt hopeless, hold on! Wonderful changes are going to happen in your life as you begin to live it on purpose. God says, *"I know what I am planning for you.... I have good plans for you, not plans to hurt you. I will give you hope and a good future.'"*[9] You may feel you are facing an impossible situation, but the Bible says, *"God ... is able to do far more than we would ever dare to ask or even dream of—infinitely beyond our highest prayers, desires, thoughts, or hopes."*[10]

Knowing your purpose simplifies your life. It defines what you do and what you don't do. Your purpose becomes the standard you use to evaluate which activities are essential and which aren't. You simply ask, "Does this activity help me fulfill one of God's purposes for my life?"

Without a clear purpose you have no foundation on which you base decisions, allocate your time, and use your resources. You will tend to make choices based on circumstances, pressures, and your mood at that moment. People who don't know their purpose try to do too much—and *that* causes stress, fatigue, and conflict.

It is impossible to do everything people want you to do. You have just enough time to do God's will. If you can't get it all done, it means you're trying to do more than God intended for you to do (or, possibly, that you're watching too much television). Purpose-driven living leads to a simpler lifestyle and a saner schedule. The Bible says, *"A pretentious, showy life is an empty life; a plain and simple life is a full life."*[11] It also leads to peace of mind: *"You, LORD, give perfect peace to those who keep their purpose firm and put their trust in you."* [12]

Knowing your purpose focuses your life. It concentrates your effort and energy on what's important. You become effective by being selective.

It's human nature to get distracted by minor issues. We play *Trivial Pursuit* with our lives. Henry David Thoreau observed that people live lives of *"quiet desperation,"* but today a better description is *aimless distraction*. Many people are like gyroscopes, spinning around at a frantic pace but never going anywhere.

Without a clear purpose, you will keep changing directions, jobs, relationships, churches, or other externals—hoping each change will settle the confusion or fill the emptiness in your heart. You think, *Maybe this time it will be different,* but it doesn't solve your real problem—a lack of focus and purpose.

The Bible says, *"Don't live carelessly, unthinkingly. Make sure you understand what the Master wants."* [13]

The power of focusing can be seen in light. Diffused light has little power or impact, but you can concentrate its energy by focusing it. With a magnifying glass, the rays of the sun can be focused to set grass or paper on fire. When light is focused even more as a laser beam, it can cut through steel.

If you want your life to have impact, focus it!

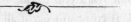

There is nothing quite as potent as a focused life, one lived on purpose. The men and women who have made the greatest difference in history were the most focused. For instance, the apostle Paul almost single-handedly spread Christianity throughout the Roman Empire. His secret was a focused life. He said, *"I am focusing all my energies on this one thing: Forgetting the past and looking forward to what lies ahead."* [14]

If you want your life to have impact, *focus* it! Stop dabbling. Stop trying to do it all. Do less. Prune away even good activities and do only that which matters most. Never confuse activity with productivity. You can be busy without a purpose, but what's the point? Paul said, *"Let's keep focused on that goal, those of us who want everything God has for us."* [15]

Knowing your purpose motivates your life. Purpose always produces passion. Nothing energizes like a clear purpose. On the other hand, passion dissipates when you lack a purpose. Just getting out of bed becomes a major chore. It is usually meaningless work, not overwork, that wears us down, saps our strength, and robs our joy.

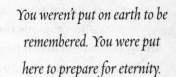

You weren't put on earth to be remembered. You were put here to prepare for eternity.

George Bernard Shaw wrote, "This is the true joy of life: the being used up for a purpose recognized by yourself as a mighty one; being a force of nature instead of a feverish, selfish little clot of ailments and grievances, complaining that the world will not devote itself to making you happy."

Knowing your purpose prepares you for eternity. Many people spend their lives trying to create a lasting legacy on earth. They want to be remembered when they're gone. Yet, what ultimately matters most will not be what others say about your life but what *God* says. What people fail to realize is that all achievements are eventually surpassed, records are broken, reputations fade, and tributes are forgotten. In college, James Dobson's goal was to become the school's tennis champion. He felt proud when his trophy was prominently placed in the school's trophy cabinet. Years later, someone mailed him that trophy. They had found it in a trashcan when the school was remodeled. Jim said, *"Given enough time, all your trophies will be trashed by someone else!"*

Living to create an earthly legacy is a short-sighted goal. A wiser use of time is to build an *eternal* legacy. You weren't put on earth to be remembered. You were put here to prepare for eternity.

One day you will stand before God, and he will do an audit of your life, a final exam, before you enter eternity. The Bible says, *"Remember, each of us will stand personally before the judgment seat of God.... Yes, each of us will have to give a personal account to God."*[16] Fortunately, God wants us to pass this test, so he has given us the questions in advance. From the Bible we can surmise that God will ask us two crucial questions:

First, *"What did you do with my Son, Jesus Christ?"* God won't ask about your religious background or doctrinal views. The only thing that will matter is, did you accept what Jesus did for you and did you learn to love and trust him? Jesus said, *"I am the way and the truth and the life. No one comes to the Father except through me."*[17]

Second, *"What did you do with what I gave you?"* What did you do with your life—all the gifts, talents, opportunities, energy, relationships, and resources God gave you? Did you spend them on yourself, or did you use them for the purposes God made you for?"

Preparing you for these two questions is the goal of this book. The first question will determine *where* you spend eternity. The second question will determine *what you do* in eternity. By the end of this book you will be ready to answer both questions.

Point to Ponder: Living on purpose is the path to peace.

Verse to Remember: *"You, LORD, give perfect peace to those who keep their purpose firm and put their trust in you."* Isaiah 26:3 (TEV)

Question to Consider: What would my family and friends say is the driving force of my life? What do I want it to be?

NOTES

Day 1: It All Starts with God
1. Job 12:10 (TEV).
2. Romans 8:6 (Msg).
3. Matthew 16:25 (Msg).
4. Hugh S. Moorhead, comp., *The Meaning of Life According to Our Century's Greatest Writers and Thinkers* (Chicago: Chicago Review Press, 1988).
5. 1 Corinthians 2:7 (Msg).
6. Ephesians 1:11 (Msg).
7. David Friend, ed., *The Meaning of Life* (Boston: Little, Brown, 1991), 194.

Day 2: You Are Not an Accident
1. Psalm 138:8a (NIV).
2. Psalm 139:15 (Msg).
3. Psalm 139:16 (LB).
4. Acts 17:26 (NIV).
5. Ephesians 1:4a (Msg).
6. James 1:18 (NCV).
7. Michael Denton, *Nature's Destiny: How the Laws of Biology Reveal Purpose in the Universe* (New York: Free Press, 1998), 389.
8. Isaiah 45:18 (GWT).
9. 1 John 4:8
10. Isaiah 46:3–4 (NCV).
11. Russell Kelfer. Used by permission.

Day 3: What Drives Your Life?
1. Genesis 4:12 (NIV).
2. Psalm 32:1 (LB).
3. Job 5:2 (TEV).
4. 1 John 4:18 (Msg).
5. Matthew 6:24 (NLT).
6. Isaiah 49:4 (NIV).
7. Job 7:6 (LB).
8. Job 7:16 (TEV).
9. Jeremiah 29:11 (NCV).
10. Ephesians 3:20 (LB).
11. Proverbs 13:7 (Msg).
12. Isaiah 26:3 (TEV).
13. Ephesians 5:17 (Msg).
14. Philippians 3:13 (NLT).
15. Philippians 3:15 (Msg).
16. Romans 14:10b, 12 (NLT).
17. John 14:6 (NIV).

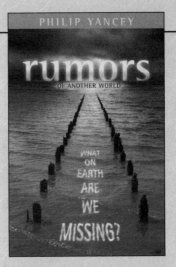

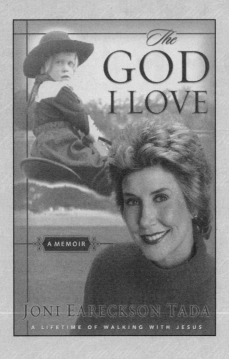

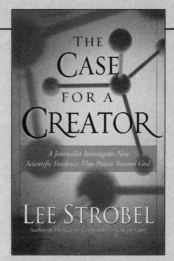

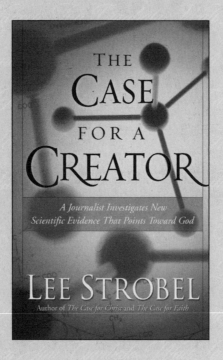

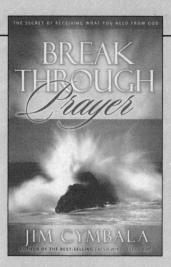

SPECIAL OFFER

see below for details

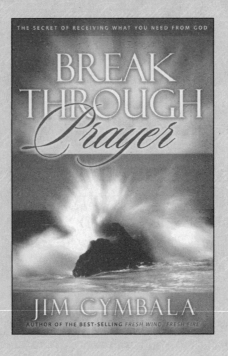

Customer: Redeemable only at participating bookstores. Not redeemable through Zondervan. Coupon may not be reproduced. Limit one per customer, please. Not valid with any other offers. Offer expires December 30, 2003.

Retailer: Customer is eligible for $3.00 off *Breakthrough Prayer* with this coupon. Please redeem with your next Zondervan payment for $1.50 credit. Must redeem by January 31, 2004.

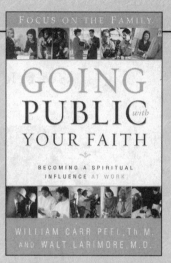

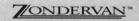

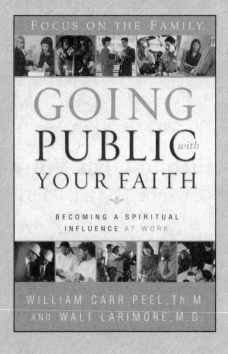

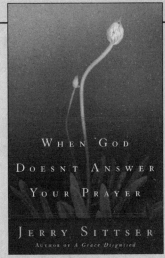

SPECIAL OFFER

see below for details

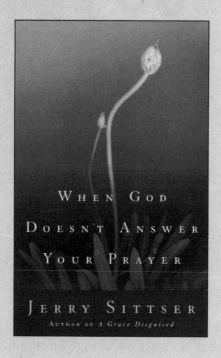

Customer: Redeemable only at participating bookstores. Not redeemable through Zondervan. Coupon may not be reproduced. Limit one per customer, please. Not valid with any other offers. Offer expires March 5, 2004.

Retailer: Customer is eligible for $3.00 off *When God Doesn't Answer Your Prayer* with this coupon. Please redeem with your next Zondervan payment for $1.50 credit. Must redeem by April 5, 2004.

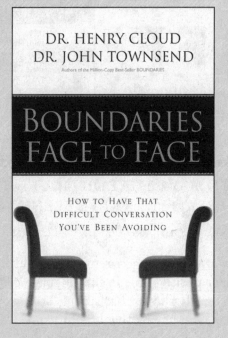

SPECIAL OFFER

see below for details

Customer: Redeemable only at participating bookstores. Not redeemable through Zondervan. Coupon may not be reproduced. Limit one per customer, please. Not valid with any other offers. Offer expires January 15, 2004.

Retailer: Customer is eligible for $5.00 off any edition of Zondervan's *NIV Student Bible* with this coupon. Please redeem with your next Zondervan payment for $2.50 credit. Must redeem by February 15, 2004.

We want to hear from you. Please send your comments about this book to us in care of zreview@zondervan.com. Thank you.

GRAND RAPIDS, MICHIGAN 49530 USA

WWW.ZONDERVAN.COM